FINANCING INFORMATION SERVICES

FINANCING INFORMATION SERVICES

Problems, Changing Approaches, and New Opportunities for Academic and Research Libraries

Edited by
PETER SPYERS-DURAN
and
THOMAS W. MANN, JR.

New Directions in Librarianship, Number 6

Greenwood Press
Westport, Connecticut · London, England

Library of Congress Cataloging in Publication Data

Main entry under title:

Financing information services.

(New directions in librarianship, ISSN 0147-1090; no. 6)
Bibliography: p.
Includes index.
1. Libraries, University and college—Finance—
Addresses, essays, lectures. 2. Research libraries—
Finance—Addresses, essays, lectures. 3. Information
services—Finance—Addresses, essays, lectures.
I. Spyers-Duran, Peter. II. Mann, Thomas W. III. Series.
Z675.U5F56 1985   027.7   84-15729
ISBN 0-313-24644-0 (lib. bdg.)

Library of Congress Catalog Card Number: 84-15729
ISBN: 0-313-24644-0
ISSN: 0147-1090

First published in 1985

Greenwood Press
A division of Congressional Information Service, Inc.
88 Post Road West
Westport, Connecticut 06881

Printed in the United States of America

10 9 8 7 6 5 4 3 2 1

Contents

III. New Opportunities

FINANCING
INFORMATION
SERVICES

Introduction

Peter Spyers-Duran and Thomas W. Mann, Jr.

The essays printed in this volume were first presented at an international conference entitled "Contemporary Issues in Academic and Research Libraries," held at Boulder, Colorado, on February 28, 29 and March 1, 1984. The distinguished speakers and registrants represented a wide range of expertise including librarians, presidents, academic administrators, computer experts, and business executives from England, Canada, Australia, and the United States.

The conference papers raised many issues and questions stimulating and challenging the profession to seek new responses and new solutions to persistent and nagging issues in academic and research librarianship. The issues raised by the contributors can best be summarized by these two basic questions: Can academic and research libraries cope with the current technological, economic, and organizational issues that are bringing about rapid changes in information technology and information services? Will libraries require fundamental changes in order to remain operationally effective and economically viable? The full answer to these and other questions raised was not the purpose of the conference.

However, the reader will undoubtedly benefit from the wealth of information, advice, and experience shared by the distinguished contributors through these papers.

Because of the abundance of material, the contributed papers have been divided by topics and published as two separate volumes, each with its own distinct title. The companion volume to this work is entitled *Issues in Academic Librarianship: Views and Case Studies for the 1980s and 1990s.*

The first essay of this volume written by Sigmund Ginsburg provides thought-provoking material on the general financial environment facing institutions and proposes several specific and sometimes drastic actions that an institution might be able to consider to avoid financial disaster.

S. B. Saul describes the erosion of the funding levels of British university libraries, further aggravated by the high cost of U.S. dollars, especially in those areas of library acquisitions where there is a heavy dependence on U.S. publishers.

Ed Johnson's paper on financial planning takes issue with Mr. Ginsburg who suggested that financial retrenchments should be planned with care.

The views of an academic administrator are given in the paper of Maurice Glicksman, outlining the importance of scholarly resource sharing and the necessity of attention to the proper application of information technology.

Paul Kantor discusses his recent survey and research study of the relations between cost and services in academic libraries. He has found that library budgets do not necessarily reflect service burdens of the libraries. Instead, total budgets are statistically strongly related to the total holdings.

Dan Lester reviews the last twenty years of academic funding formulas. It is clear that the Clapp–Jordan formula made a major impact on formula budgeting practices. It is also clear that the search for an ideal formula is still in process.

Murray Martin suggests that libraries will be increasingly part of the information industries. As such, new financial planning tools will be needed to reflect the shift of resource needs from acquisition of materials to the contract services of databases and the like.

Sherm Hayes makes a case for total resource budget planning that includes not only the base budget of the library but also other income potential from gifts and grants.

The final section of this book explores new opportunities for academic and research libraries.

David Weber and Richard McCoy's joint paper explores some of the more salient features of current library automation, noting that technological developments show no sign of slowing.

JoAn Segal defines the sometimes misunderstood term "networks" and discusses a certain level and kind of network which provides services to its members largely in the field of cooperation and automation.

Nina Cohen is one of a new breed of enterprising librarians offering an option to libraries to get certain jobs done through external contracting. Her chapter identifies tasks such as binding, shelving, or cataloging which might be advantageous for contracting out by the library.

Ted Welch describes an increasingly important grantsmanship process and offers valuable suggestions on ways to attract donor dollars.

The views and opinions expressed in these essays are not necessarily endorsed by the editors. However, the importance of these papers is great as they will influence future academic and research library development for years to come.

I

PROBLEMS

1

Austerity in Higher Education: Problems and Opportunities

Sigmund G. Ginsburg

Practically all higher education institutions are dealing with or will have to deal with significant to severe austerity for about the next decade. In facing the difficult issues and efforts involved, an institution has the opportunity to meet the challenges and emerge at least as strong as it was before. Success in meeting the formidable challenges will require realistic planners who are willing and able to depart from approaches and traditions of the past, a great deal of cooperation among faculty, administrators, trustees and others, and considerable skill in implementation and evaluation of results with modifications made as necessary. While success in living with austerity and easing its strains can be expected for the next few decades, money will never be plentiful, and an emphasis on effectiveness, efficiency, and sound management will always be necessary.

My focus is on what administrators and those involved with higher education can do, but we must not overlook the impact on our primary "customers": the students and their parents.

For many parents, providing higher education for their children represents the greatest outlay of funds in a family's budget, exceeding even the cost of home ownership. Depending upon the number of children, the number of years of higher education, the field of interest, the college selected, and the total expenses (tuition, books, travel, room, board, living expenses), the cost can be as much as $200,000. It is no wonder then that the disposable income of families and their savings can be decimated in order to provide a good education for their children, even at lower cost public universities. It is not unusual for a college graduate to emerge with a bachelor's degree and $10,000–$15,000 in debts to pay for the education, with perhaps double the debt after going through law or medical school.

THE ENVIRONMENT FOR HIGHER EDUCATION

The higher education environment is highlighted by several of the following factors.

— Declining enrollments.

— Declining federal support in most areas of research and in student financial aid in terms of noninflated dollars or absolute dollars, thus limiting access to college and placing greater financial strain on institutional and personal resources.

— Inadequate state funding for public institutions in most states owing to the economic problems.

— Increased competition for students between and among public and independent two and four year institutions and from company training programs and proprietary institutions.

— Increased competition among and within institutions for funding from government, business and industry, foundations and private sources and for allocation of funds within an institution.

— Increased competition and tension in regard to funding the academic areas versus the nonacademic areas.

— Increased costs to upgrade and replace instructional, research, and administrative equipment; preserve and replace deteriorating library books; provide adequate computer equipment for instruction and research; meet long delayed, deferred maintenance needs; upgrade, replace, and refurbish existing buildings and facilities.

— Increased concern about the mission of the institution and what constitutes an educated person—career vs. liberal arts/humanities education.

— The probability of continuing inflation in higher education, somewhat higher than the general economy because of education's high labor intensity and little likelihood of employing machinery and technology to increase productivity.

— Continuing need and costs for higher education in making up for the deficiencies or gaps in the education offered by many high schools.

— Increased concern about human rights as well as political or social issues involved in a university's investment policies and their impact on returns received from investments.

— Increased competition among institutions for outstanding faculty and administrators with less opportunity for mobility for those who are less than very good or outstanding. Increased difficulty in recruiting and retaining outstanding faculty in specific areas where industry offers considerably more compensation and modern equipment and research support, for example, engineering, computer science, and physical sciences.

— The increasing financial burden of accountability, environmental and social legislation, and regulation.

— Financial pressures causing boards of trustees to be more concerned about all of the above and in public institutions; increased concern by governmental agencies and the legislatures.

— Increasing concern about morale, productivity, and a good working and educational atmosphere on campus as a result of faculty and staff recognizing that because of the factors mentioned above, advancement and salary increase opportunities at the institution and mobility outside the institution are less than in the past; job security is less certain, and funding to enrich, enlarge, or create new programs, services, or systems, or to provide even the basics can be in serious question.

In addition, higher education faces concerns about: volatility in the economy and in political support, changing values and life-styles, more frequent job and career changes, career education versus liberal arts education (or what some would call hire education versus higher education), legal and moral requirements in regard to affirmative action, shortages of qualified high school teachers of science and mathematics.

Within each institution there may be a need to focus more sharply on evaluating its mission, defining what constitutes higher education, and effectiveness, efficiency, and economy in managing an institution, including concern for planning and organization, student and staff satisfaction, marketing and public relations.

As a result of all the above, many institutions will face austerity and some will face financial exigency. Some institutions will go bankrupt and disappear, and others will merge with stronger institutions or significantly change their orientations from independent to public, from four year to two year, or from liberal arts to technical or career oriented.

WHAT CAN BE DONE

I shall deal specifically with what can be done at an institutional level, but it is helpful to broaden the scope and look at five groups that are of great importance in focusing on the problems of higher education.

Government Officials

Federal officials and legislators should be concerned about appropriate levels of student financial aid, loans, graduate research, assistantships, research awards, assistance in upgrading facilities and equipment, and the burdens of governmental regulations. Governors, legislators, state boards of regents or departments of education must become concerned about the proliferation of campuses, duplication of programs, and high standards of quality, effectiveness, and efficiency. If public and private institutions are not able to take action on their own, then the state must step in, particularly in regard to public institutions. Of course, adequate state financial support is important, but the state should be concerned about what steps each institution is taking to appropriately allocate state funds. For example, in some states, there are simply too many public two and four year institutions. In Ohio, there are 57 accredited private colleges, 39 public institutions, 23 university branches, eight community colleges and 17 technical colleges, and seven medical colleges. Since 1963, Ohio has expanded from six state public universities to 12. Indiana, with half the population, has four. In Ohio, the campuses and branches were built in order to have a campus within 30 miles of every student. (One branch of a public university created as a favor to a former legislator has only about 150 full-time equivalent students.) That has a profound impact, affecting expenditures for construction, debt service, maintenance and operation of physical plant, funds available for faculty and staff salaries, instructional and research equipment, library materials, and the like. Ohio has spent two hundred million dollars since 1969 to build four new medical colleges and expand three others. At the time they were being built, there were serious questions as to whether the new medical colleges were necessary, but political factors, power, and prestige prevailed.

Funding too many institutions is a drain on the state and does not allow sufficient resources to build good or outstanding institutions. It also means higher tuition paid by students since state support is inadequate. Thus, some institutions need to be closed. But there is political pressure to prevent closings. At various institutions there are program duplications; some should be eliminated since they are low quality and costly, but again there is pressure against this. Sometimes buildings are built that are not necessary, but a legislator's name may be on the building, and there is political value in construction jobs.

Trustees

Trustees perform a vital function in terms of broad policy-making for the institution. Many trustees are knowledgeable and truly dedicated to the particular institution or, at state board of regents levels, to higher education. However, in some states, a few appointments to a board are a prestigious form of patronage. Thus, higher education as a whole as well as each institution needs to have the governor appoint those who are leaders in their field, who have the time, capacity, and interest to devote themselves to higher education issues and to the broad policy issues of the institution. For independent institutions, the same needs exist. A major function of trustees is to require the administration to provide a specific plan as to how the institution intends to face future problems and opportunities.

The Administration

The third group is the administration—the president, vice presidents, and deans—working with various groups in the institution, comprising faculty leadership, staff leadership, students, and union leaders. They must focus on the academic and financial future of the institution and the actions necessary to maintain financial viability, quality of effort, and reasonable costs. At particular institutions there is often a proliferation and duplication of programs and courses and the various support services connected with such programs. Considerable progress has been made in the last decade in improving the management of higher education, but there is much that remains to be done. In addition to concern for academic values and quality, there must be a concern for sound management planning and practice and an emphasis on marketing, customer satisfaction, effectiveness, efficiency, and economy.

The Faculty

Since the academic mission is central to any institution, the understanding, involvement, and support of the faculty in regard to controlling costs is of great importance. Their ideas, their concern, and their commitment, as an entire group and within departments and colleges, can be one vital factor in bringing about changes.

The "Customers" of Higher Education and Its Contributors

Students and their parents as customers, and foundations, corporations, alumni, and friends as contributors, should be concerned about the quality, cost, and value of the education offered at the institution, and they should make their views known to the administration, trustees, and state officials. In effect, students can "vote" by not going to the institution and contributors by not contributing.

Fundamental to dealing with the difficult times ahead is the necessity for a full understanding of the challenge of living with austerity. We must have the courage and determination to meet the problem sooner than later, to use a scalpel rather than a hatchet. More money from public or private sources, foundations, companies, alumni, and unanticipated bequests may come along, but one cannot count on it. Thus, each institution must take stock of itself, its past and present, where it wants to go, and how it intends to get there. The analysis must be made realistically and conservatively, with determination to take the necessary difficult actions.

Success in this endeavor requires trust, cooperation, and a strong sense of community, of individuals banding together to confront a potentially fatal crisis. It is essential to realize that admitting that a crisis is at hand is not pessimism, or crying wolf, but recognition of risk for an institution's quality and mission. After it has been established that there is a clear and present danger to the heart and soul of the institution, efforts must be made to build a community of interest in taking action. The common tendency in academe to engage in wishful thinking must be overcome. Administrators, faculty members, trustees, students, alumni, and state agencies must pull together as a team to meet the crisis. The usual and normal vested interests, rivalries, and the litany of past or present errors must be put aside to face the present and future dangers. A financial exigency planning task force, with committees and involvement of various constituencies such as trustees, faculty and staff members, administrators, and alumni, with full sharing of ideas and information, will be necessary. There must be a willingness to question how and why things are done and what path the institution is following, to dare to dream things that never were and to say, why not. An institution might have to open up all its books and look at its weaknesses and dirty linen, as well as its strengths and aspirations. Everything should be questioned, and the usual turf prerogatives will have to go by the wayside. Trustees and nonacademic administrators will have to be free to ask academic leaders and faculty members tough questions about practices, procedures, and philosophy and, at the same time, be prepared to answer tough questions.

Administrators and trustees, like everyone else, get trapped by traditions of the past. They, too, will have to consider unconventional means to meet the crisis. Certainly waste, errors, wrong expenditures, and poor financial and program investments will come to light. Although these are important to an understanding of the financial plight an institution faces, the most important stage lies ahead. After the problem is recognized and analyzed and possible solutions are examined, the next step is to choose a general strategy for staving off exigency and building a better tomorrow. That kind of thinking requires intellectual and moral honesty, creativity, and a sense of dedication to the institution rather than to a singular constituency or position. Out of this approach can come new missions, programs, services, managerial styles, organizational and governance arrangements and communications.

In reaching and implementing decisions, those whose involvement, ability, and dedication are most critical to success are: the board of trustees and its various committees, particularly the executive and planning committees, the president and vice presidents, the deans, the faculty senate, and the leaders of the employee groups or unions, particularly of the faculty. There will be extreme pressures on union leaders and faculty senate leaders to uphold usual positions and methods of doing things. Success in avoiding financial exigency may depend on the ability to withstand the pressure, to think of the future of the institution as a whole, and to rethink traditional practices. Contracts, personnel plans, and agreements may have to be reopened and changed in order to bring about immediate, short-term, and long-term reduced costs.

Involvement must extend beyond the leaders, however. All those affected should be fully informed and have an opportunity to express their views before decisive action is taken. Ultimately, the responsibility and authority for final decision-making is in the hands of the trustees, acting on the recommendations of the president, but true and lasting success in dealing with the problem will depend on openness and full discussion with everyone affected.

I offer for your consideration 50 ways to overcome present or potential austerity by increasing income and decreasing expenses. Some of the ideas will not be appropriate for particular institutions or have already been tried, others will need significant modification. They are offered as a stimulus to thinking about specific actions that might be considered. Each will be difficult to plan and implement. With luck, only a few will be necessary. But these and other ideas must be considered in a careful, rational, planned way, rather than causing a great upheaval by reacting at the last possible minute and thereby increasing the chances of failure.

In developing the list, I have assumed that there is agreement as to the primacy of academic programs and services and that most institutions will not be able to afford a smorgasbord of programs and courses. It is also understood that there will be a goal of selective excellence in academic programs and choices to be made considering quality, centrality to academic missions, current and future potential in academic and support programs, and quality and scope of service to the community, region, and nation.

I have also emphasized the need to be concerned with cost effectiveness; a marketing, public relations, and service orientation; creativity, innovation, and a concern for competition; careful evaluation of existing philosophies, policies, programs, and practices corresponding to present and future needs and a changing environment. Although these considerations are more economic than academic, they are important.

Planners must be mindful of the fact that it takes many years to build a solid reputation for academic quality. That reputation can be downgraded sharply or destroyed in less than a decade. Thus, any actions taken must emphasize the need to protect and, if possible, advance the academic core and future of the institution.

INCREASING INCOME

1. Increase fund-raising results through creative approaches and new gift-giving vehicles and through emphasis on effectiveness and efficiency. Make a concerted effort to improve alumni relations and increase contact with alumni as a means to maintain or in-

crease enrollment and fund-raising. Use alumni contacts for enrollment and foundation, business and general fund-raising from those not previously associated with the institution.

2. Improve public relations and increase media attention in regard to academic quality, research capability, public service, human relations, student services, and a "good-place-to-enroll" image of the university to improve enrollment, reputation, research grants, and fund-raising.

3. Improve recruitment of students, admissions procedures, and marketing of the university. Consider various payment plans that make it more convenient for students to pay their bills, for example, use of credit cards, deferred payment plans, various loan arrangements, prepayment of four years of tuition without any increase in tuition. Emphasize retention of students.

4. Review scholarship, loan and work study opportunities, policies and programs to encourage increased enrollment or to maintain enrollment and retention, and attempt to get additional funding for scholarships and loans.

5. Increase the number of programs, courses or services geared to needs of business, industry, government, and other groups to increase enrollment and income.

6. Increase research geared to needs of business, industry, government, and other institutions, thus increasing direct income and overhead. Consider establishing joint research ventures with business, industry, and other institutions. Provide encouragement and incentives to individuals and units to develop research, grant, contract and funding proposals to the government, business, and industry foundations and other sources.

7. Seek ways to obtain instructional and administrative equipment, supplies, books, and materials from various vendors either as a means for such companies to make contributions, enhance their own reputations, and use the institution as a pilot demonstration or to arrive at some form of barter arrangement for university services and research.

8. Attempt to predict receptivity to or need for approaches, methods, services, degrees, courses, programs, and majors not presently given at the institution or nearby institutions, and develop and market these ahead of other institutions. This requires some insights and investments in regard to the future needs of the area, region, or nation and positioning the institution to be at the forefront of meeting these needs.

9. Increase programs, courses, services, and methods of education geared to the adult, nontraditional and continuing education markets. Focus on time, place, type and method of instruction and special services and incentives in order to attract new students.

10. Emphasize television and cable television, cassette, computer instruction, and other applications of technology in order to tap new markets, improve quality and productivity, and enhance the image of the institution.

11. Consider various marketing approaches and incentives to increase full- and part-time enrollment as well as enrollment in evening, summer school, and continuing education programs, for example, no-need scholarships, based on outstanding previous academic performance, partial tuition reductions if one takes "x" credits during summer school or brings in a friend or family member, partial reductions if two or more members of the immediate family attend.

12. Institute differential tuition pricing to cover additional costs in certain colleges or programs. Reduce the number of credits covered by the flat tuition rate.

13. Review present fees to determine whether they should be raised to cover direct and indirect costs and consider instituting new fees for such things as transcripts, laboratory supplies, student activities, filing student aid applications, loans, late payments, graduation, and special services.

14. Attempt to increase state subsidy or at least change subsidy formulas to recognize fixed costs even with declining enrollments.

15. Review investment, financing, and money management policies, strategies, and techniques to bring about changes that meet the institution's needs, short-term and long-term. Explore use of investment vehicles that may not have been used by the institution: options, futures, stock lending, real estate, venture capital, investment in businesses, foreign investments, and various money management techniques. Consider financing through such means as loans, bonds, bond anticipation notes, certificates of participation. Emphasize ways in which the tax laws provide incentives to business and lending institutions to provide funding or equipment to higher education institutions. Change investment portfolio, sacrificing growth to some extent, but gaining greater income. This might allow reducing general funds support to areas that get increased income from the investment policy change.

16. Use total funds approach to budgeting, thereby reducing general funds expenditures by using other funds available to units. In such an approach, consider the expendable portions of endowment funds as well as the interest earned on the endowment, existing quasi-endowment, restricted and gift funds, and the interest they earn.

17. Review possibilities for increasing revenue generating activities by selling space, specific services or skills, for example, computer services, printing, consulting, research, and technical assistance. Institutions should recognize the possibility of complaints from community suppliers of such services and the impact on the university's reputation and also be aware of unrelated business income tax implications.

18. Form private practice corporations similar to those in a medical center to generate additional income for faculty and the university. This may apply to areas such as engineering, law, architecture, management, chemistry, or physics.

19. Review patent policy of the university to maximize possible returns to faculty members and the university as a result of research performed.

20. Sell, rent, or lease university land, fine arts, properties and other assets that are not needed.

DECREASING EXPENSES

1. Reduce the number of positions through freezing vacancies, instituting early retirement programs, eliminating positions, combining units, and job enrichment and enlargement.

2. Moderate salary increases, or if necessary freeze salaries for a year or two or reduce salaries, or substitute pickup of retirement costs which give employees more take home pay as compared with the same percentage salary increase.

3. Evaluate fringe benefit costs, and reduce benefits or have employees bear a greater share of the cost.

4. Increase student employment as a lower cost substitute for full- or part-time employees and as a means of generating income for students, thus helping enrollment and retention.

5. Where possible, employ part-time employees or nine- or ten-month employees rather than full-time employees to reduce salary and

fringe benefit costs. Emphasize flex time approaches and job sharing in order to reduce personnel costs; encourage leave without pay.

6. Reduce, phase out, and eliminate expenditures for nonacademic units, functions, services, and activities that are not essential to support the basic academic missions of the institution. The above actions and merging of separate units will reduce managerial, staffing, and support costs and will also reduce space needs and costs.

7. Emphasize use of new instructional and administrative equipment, technology, techniques, and systems in order to reduce personnel and other costs, increase productivity, and improve service.

8. Review university organization and hierarchy to determine if some units or positions can be eliminated or consolidated, thereby reducing the number of positions at all levels, including middle, upper, and top administration. There may be too many high ranking individuals and too few staff.

9. Increase productivity by: reducing paperwork and red tape; encouraging delegation, job enrichment and enlargement; combining units; reducing hierarchy; rewarding merit, thus reducing the need for overtime, part-time staff, and allowing the elimination of positions. Review time spent on various functions to determine if these functions can be eliminated or reduced, or procedures and policies improved leading to reduced work effort, thereby eliminating staff, reducing the number of full and part-time staff, or freeing staff to take on other duties.

10. Reduce the number and level of services and activities provided.

11. Set higher performance standards in regard to salary increases and renewal of administrative and academic contracts. Implement effective performance evaluation systems and goal setting for all staff, including tenured staff. Award salary increases predominantly on merit based upon the performance evaluation.

12. Reduce the number of courses and sections and the number of small classes, thereby eliminating some overload and adjunct faculty costs and possibly the need for some full-time positions. Reduce duplication of courses, that is, similar courses given in two or more colleges or departments.

13. Increase the number of courses taught by each faculty member and number of student credit hours generated through: more

courses taught per year, larger classes, evening, overload or summer school courses regarded as part of a larger base load—thereby eliminating part-time and full-time positions.

14. Develop ways to insure that academic freedom is maintained. Develop ways to evaluate tenured faculty and to take action, in a timely manner, with careful protection to the individual, in those cases where actions such as counseling, retraining, salary freeze, probation, leave of absence, and dismissal are necessary. Review impact on tenured faculty of program reduction, phase out or discontinuation. Develop a system of non–tenure track positions in addition to the existing tenure system.

15. Tighten standards for granting tenure, promotion, and renewal of contracts; consider program and financial implications and projections in addition to individual merit, as important aspects of the decisions to be reached; consider caps on number of tenured positions and various levels of full-time positions.

16. Reduce expenditures and combine, phase out, or eliminate academic majors, programs, units, services, and activities that are not:

    a. central to the mission of the institution

    b. of major importance to the institution; and

    c. of high quality or low cost where there is little likelihood that the institution could afford to raise the quality or generate income to offset costs.

    In essence, spend resources only on those areas that are of great importance; do not spread resources too far. Bolster and support the good, potentially good, and required rather than bringing everything to a level of mediocrity. Prune, and use a scalpel now rather than having to swing a hatchet later.

17. Cross-train faculty so that those who have fewer students or courses because of enrollment trends can teach in other areas where there is ample enrollment. This would reduce the need for new full-time faculty or for adjunct faculty.

18. Change the academic calendar if this would help enrollment, energy, or administrative costs, and not be a detriment to fulfilling the academic mission.

19. Emphasize inter-library loans, use of technology, and other means of cost savings in order to reduce library expenditures.

20. Reduce costs for intercollegiate athletics.

21. Emphasize competitive bidding for goods and services. Explore with other institutions joint buying of goods and services in order to lower costs; explore with other educational institutions sharing of library, transportation, maintenance and instructional equipment, classroom, laboratory, and other facilities, perhaps sharing the costs of faculty or specialized administrators in particular specialties where neither school needs a full-time appointee or arrange to minimize duplicating each other's programs, thus reducing expense.

22. Contract out certain support services, such as food service, bookstore, maintenance, cleaning, and security. Alternatively, if currently contracting out, explore advantages/disadvantages of performing the services.

23. Reduce or eliminate external consultants, expert assistance, and outside services: use faculty, if possible, or build internal staffs if this is cost effective and meets the needs, for example, legal services.

24. Emphasize economy, planning, efficiency, and care in use of supplies, paper, telephone, duplicating, mail, advertising, printing, and reduce expenditures in these areas.

25. Emphasize energy and utility cost savings throughout the institution through conservation, controls, and new technology, including not only major items such as heating or cooling buildings or upgrading or converting boilers for multiple fuel use, but also smaller items such as shutting off lights, reducing use of elevators, and decreasing the number of fans or heaters.

26. Computerize more systems, thereby reducing the number of staff necessary.

27. Reduce new construction and operating costs associated with new space by utilizing existing space more hours per week, weeks per year, and if necessary, renting space off campus or using high schools, libraries, and similar institutions for classroom space.

28. Close campus or individual buildings at certain times in order to save utility and maintenance costs; vacations should be taken at the time buildings are closed.

29. Coordinate and reduce advertising, publication, and printing expenses; convince advertisers to pay for certain publications; sell advertising in alumni and other publications.

30. Encourage implementation of an effective suggestion system to

focus on decreasing expenses, increasing income, and increasing productivity.

Higher education faces some very difficult times ahead. College administrators need support and understanding from faculty colleagues and from those outside the field who recognize the importance of higher education to our country and society, now and in the future.

All of us in higher education need to have personal courage and determination to look at why and how we do things, to question past practices, and to plan ahead for the future. We must recognize that although higher education is indeed different from business, industry, and government, legitimate questions can be raised in regard to the management of an institution, the quality of programs and services rendered, the concern for creativity, customer service, and satisfaction. I believe it is imperative for this nation to place higher priority on adequately funding colleges and universities directly and indirectly by promoting access to higher education through scholarships, loans, and work study opportunities. At the same time, it is imperative for us in higher education to be concerned about the most effective and efficient use of the resources available to us.

As we go about the very difficult task of planning to meet or avoid austerity we must recognize that excellent plans are often ineffective because of poor implementation. In the implementation stage there should be anticipation of the careful planning necessary and the difficulties involved as well as the consideration of the impact on morale and people's lives. Long- and short-run implementation and results must be considered as well as methods of encouraging full cooperation.

Once the immediate or looming crisis appears to have passed, constant vigilance is needed. Continuing evaluation, planning, discussion, and involvement of the various constituencies are necessary. A very valuable by-product of successfully dealing with the financial crisis is the probability of an improvement in the sense of community on campus and in relations between faculty and administration, administration and board, and faculty and board, and in the case of public institutions, relations with state agencies.

Improved resource allocation and the suggestions set forth above can result in a leaner but better institution with more funds available for salaries, research support, student services, facilities, instructional equipment and library materials, and innovative programs and approaches. For many students and their families the end result could be a higher quality education that is affordable.

Higher education faces what will probably be the toughest years it has had so far. The task is indeed formidable and perhaps overwhelming: to work together as colleagues on extremely complex problems in order to meet the challenges of austerity. If we in higher education are to strengthen our institutions now and for the future, we must offer the highest quality in lifelong education, research, and public service to our students, alumni, community, professional disciplines, region, and nation. With understanding, determination, courage, cooperation, and planning, we can indeed overcome austerity and enter into a new and brighter era for higher education.

NOTES

Some of the ideas listed in this chapter are based on or are modifications or extensions of some ideas listed in *Managing the Higher Education Enterprise*, by Nathaniel H. Karol and Sigmund G. Ginsburg, Ronald Press, New York, 1980; Budget Task Force Report, University of Cincinnati, January, 1982 (this special Task Force consisted of representatives of the Faculty Senate, Faculty and Staff Unions, Administration, Deans, Students, Staff, and other groups); "120 Ways to Increase Income and Decrease Expenses," by Sigmund G. Ginsburg, *The NACUBO Business Officer*, December, 1982; "Avoiding Financial Exigency," by Sigmund G. Ginsburg, *Educational Record*, Summer 1983.

1. The points listed are based upon or are modifications of material appearing in my article, "Avoiding Financial Exigency," *Educational Record*, Summer 1983.

2

Libraries and Austerity in Higher Education

Samuel B. Saul

Apart from the fees paid by overseas students, funding for British universities is provided almost entirely by the government, partly through home student fees whose level and extent is set by government but mainly by direct grants distributed by the University Grants Committee (UGC) which determines, and in some small measure directs, the use of the money available for each individual institution. Large capital grants for buildings, including extensions to libraries, are directly controlled by the UGC, though universities are free to make their own decisions as to the funds they wish to devote to minor works. Funds are available from private sources for library acquisitions but excluding the very special position of the libraries of Oxford and Cambridge, such donations are so small or so specialized that we can ignore them for the purposes of the present discussion. It should be remembered too, that by the standards of many American institutions, British universities are relatively small, ranging from 14,000 to 3,000 students, and in a purely economic sense this might be considered wasteful of library resources. The general position seems to be that whereas staff-student ratios at undergraduate level are generous by international standards, libraries in general are less favorably treated.

The universities have suffered a steady reduction in the real

value of their recurrent funds per student since 1975, for the
most part a period of high inflation. The increase in the numbers of students cushioned the effects until 1981 when very
severe actual cuts in funding were imposed, accompanied by
a decline in the number of undergraduate students. Over a
period of three years to August 1984 the cuts will average about
15 percent, though the reductions for particular universities
range from 0.5 percent to over 20 percent. Thus the unit of
resource—the real income per student—which in 1979/80 was
5 percent below the 1975/76 level, currently has fallen by another 11 percent. The number of full-time academic and academic related (including senior library) posts in universities
rose from 27,500 in 1970 to 34,250 in 1980 but by 1984 will
be down to 29,300.

The first attack directed specifically at libraries came in the
mid–1970s when the mounting economic difficulties of the
government resulted in a drastic reduction in the funds available to the UGC for capital construction of all kinds. At that
time twelve library projects were under serious consideration
at a cost estimated at around £12.5m, whereas the allocation
for all university building for 1976/77 was a mere £8m. It was
obvious that library buildings could not in the future be provided on anything like the former scale and the UGC set up a
working party, the Atkinson Committee, to report on the new
situation. This body was quite remarkably constrained in advance by a framework of terms of reference which dictated the
ultimate conclusions. They were instructed to make recommendations for closed access and remote storage arrangements to allow material to be placed in reserve at a rate
equivalent to the rate of accession, and to examine the possibility of discarding library material at a rate also roughly
equivalent to the rate of accession. Consequently the report,
besides reducing norms for university library space areas, also
established the concept of a self renewing library—that is, a
library of limited size in which beyond a certain point, material should be reduced at a rate approaching the level of new
purchases, though provision was made for simple reserve stores
limited to about five years acquisition. Of course, eventually
there has to be some limit to the extent to which the UGC can

finance the rate of growth of library storage space, and it must be admitted that many librarians are extremely unwilling to discard even the purest dross from their shelves. Some long-term policy was necessary, but unfortunately the Atkinson report had serious weaknesses, since it was apparently prepared to prejudice the whole function of university library provision in order to cope with a short-term difficulty. Its prime task should have been to arrive at a definition of adequate long-term physical provision for university libraries but it could do no more than base its judgment on levels of existing practice. As an example of methodology on which to base a decision of fundamental significance to universities it is breathtaking in its oversimplicity. Basically the committee's view of the rate of reduction of stock that should be achieved was far too severe and indeed came near to misunderstanding the whole point of a university library as a repository of knowledge. It is also not clear why initially the UGC decided to concentrate its capital cuts on libraries. Fortunately the hostile reception given to the Atkinson Report brought a partial change of mind and the proportion of UGC capital money devoted to libraries rose sharply to more than 40 percent—from £873k in 76/77 to £5.7m in 78/79 (34 percent of the total) and £4.5m in 1978/79 (43 percent). But the self-renewing principle is still official policy, and the University of York is trying to justify an extension in those terms even if the idea of beginning regularly to dispose of books from a library only twenty years old is manifestly absurd.

The rigidity of university budgets whereby such a large proportion of expenditures consists of salaries to staff with tenure always means that the initial response to funding cuts is to seek reductions in nonrecurrent expenditures such as building maintenance, minor works, class grants and of course library purchases. The evidence is that this has taken place on a considerable scale in British university libraries over the last decade.

The first two columns of Table 2.1 show actual spending in 1972/73 and 1981/82. The third column shows what spending in 1981/82 would have been if spending under each head had been maintained at the real level of 1972/73 and for the pur-

Table 2.1

British University Library Expenditure Pattern (in thousands of pounds)

	1 1972/73 actual spending	2 1981/82 actual spending	3 1981/82 if real level of 1972/73 maintained	4 1981/82 if real level per student of 1972/73 maintained
Salaries and wages	9034	38126	35860	45901
Books	4096	10623	15270	19546
Serials	2804	10913	10453	13380
Total	15934	59662	61583	78827

Source: University Grants Committee. Statistics.

pose uses the price index produced by the UGC—the Tress Brown index. The calculation is not entirely accurate because of changes in base rates and accounting periods but its more serious weakness is that a single index covers both books and periodicals. The rise of prices between the two dates was 273 percent for books and serials and 293 percent for wages. Column 4 is included to show that since the number of students rose by 28 percent over the two years the unit of resource for libraries fell sharply—a matter for very great concern. It will be seen from column 3 that the actual spending of 1981/82 (binding and sundries are omitted) was only a little below the real level of 1972/73. Expenditure on salaries was actually higher owing to the rectification of an old anomaly and the effects of incremental growth. Spending on serials was higher in real terms too, and all the loss fell on book purchases where real spending was reduced by a third. Detailed evidence suggests that the inflation in book prices was a little below the index average of 273 percent and periodicals a little above, but that variation was in no way enough to account for the differential rate of spending between the two. It is apparent that at a time of growing financial difficulties librarians made only very slight reductions in staff, partly because until the recent crisis staff establishments were treated separately by most universities and switching of funds between staff and acquisitions was rarely considered.

Librarians also sought to maintain their periodical runs at the expense of books. One large library for which detailed figures are available reduced the number of books purchased by a quarter between 1973/74 and 1981/82 but over the same period increased the number of periodicals taken. Of course, in some measure this trend was intensified, possibly made inevitable, by the gradual shift toward science and technology and indeed by the growth, across all the cuts, of departments in new technologies such as electronics and computer science. However, the national economic crisis reflected through rising levels of inflation and restricted funding in many areas of government spending, hit universities most powerfully in the mid–1970s. One small university library purchased 14,633 books in 1974/75 and only 9,336 in 1976/77. While the actual cost of books was unchanged over those same years, the cost of periodicals rose by two-thirds. In the larger library the purchase of books fell from 23,655 to 17,407 over the same years. The dilemma of librarians was now becoming clearer and clearer. In the small library, serials were cut back by 10 percent in 1977/78 but the gain was short-lived and book purchase continued to fall; inflation worsened and by 1980/81 book purchases were down to 7,593. This first major crisis for British universities was, however, distinctly eased by the strong level of sterling in terms of the dollar at the end of the decade as the flow of oil from the North Sea strengthened the British balance of payments. Table 2.2 measures this development through prices of periodicals over the period.

It will be seen that inflation was very rapid between 1976 and 1978 for periodicals from all sources but then slackened distinctly as American prices (in sterling terms of course) actually fell for two years, and in 1981 were still below the 1978 level. On the other hand, British prices were 60 percent higher, and those from other countries were 31 percent higher, the German mark in particular staying strong. But because of the favorable American trend the average cost of all periodicals rose by only one-quarter. Unfortunately, the dollar began to

Table 2.2

Indices of Sterling Prices of Periodicals Bought by British Libraries (1970 = 100)

	All	**U.K.**	**U.S.A.**	**Other**
1976	256	247	240	324
1978	369	336	329	473
1979	389	362	301	473
1980	412	442	296	580
1981	461	538	315	620
1982	561	633	432	710
1983	641	702	524	773

Source: Blackwell's Periodical Division. (In 1983 the sample consisted of 869 U.K., 704 U.S.A. and 434 other publications and much the same proportions obtained in other years.)

strengthen markedly just as the problems of British libraries became much more acute from 1981 onwards. The prices of American serials have risen by two-thirds over the last two years compared with 30 percent for British periodicals and one-quarter for the others. The same trends will, of course, have affected book prices, though Bowker's figures suggest that both British and American university book prices rose between 1978 and 1981 at a slightly slower rate than those of periodicals.

This prefaces the true crisis of British libraries which began in 1981 on top, be it remembered, of a long period of increasing strain. With inflation in the economy as a whole at around 20 percent universities were hard pressed throughout 1979/81, and then as late as July 1981 they were told of a catastrophic fall in income for the three years beginning in August. The decline averaged 15 percent but as regards individual institutions, it ranged from almost level funding to a loss of more than 20 percent. With such short notice there was no alternative to cutting all non-salary outgoes to the maximum degree as quickly as possible. Librarians seemed unable to resist the temptation to hold on to their serial subscriptions and books again suffered very severely. In 1981/82 over the whole system book purchase fell by 22 percent in real terms compared with the previous year. The losses were not confined to universities, of course; purchases for polytechnic libraries fell by 19 percent and for public libraries by 24 percent.

This was a vicious circle. Sales of academic books fell, unit costs and with them prices rose, and the number of volumes purchased fell even further. The reports put out by the Standing Conference of National and University Libraries (SCONUL) were dramatic indeed. Whereas in 1980/81 56 out of 57 libraries reported purchase grants which were not less in sterling than in the previous session, in 1981/82 with inflation still well in double figures, 21 reported a lower absolute grant. In 1980/81 29 libraries reported that the cuts were not affecting staffing at all; only five did so in the following year. Much the same comments were made on services. And sterling was now falling sharply. One university, savagely cut by the UGC, reported that its spending on books had dropped from £120k to £50k; periodicals had been cut in real terms by 17 percent though the sterling cost was up from £127k to £140k. This was an extreme case but the remarkable imbalance was obvious in library after library. Many universities reported cuts in the number of periodicals taken of about 10 percent though this clearly meant a higher absolute level of spending. Binding was cut back by 50 percent in many cases, hours of opening were reduced, interlibrary borrowing was rationed or charged at economic cost and some interlibrary lending was eliminated. Because computerization for libraries had to be paid for out of normal recurrent funds and not, for technical reasons, out of the equipment grants which by and large were better maintained, any real possibility of saving salary costs by new technologies were limited—in the short run anyway—by cash flow problems. The trends in the four years to 1981/82 are shown in Table 2.3 which illustrates a very large fall in the library share all together with books suffering most seriously and the rising price of periodicals coming into play again in 1981/82.

Complete disaster was avoided by two main factors. First there was the determination of university senates to protect their library acquisitions as best they could. Once the initial and unavoidable scramble for safety was over, it was obvious that the future academic strength of universities lay to a con-

Table 2.3

Share of Libraries in Total Recurrent Expenditures of English
Universities (in percentages)

	1978/79	1979/80	1980/81	1981/82
Total	5.38	5.10	4.93	4.81
Salaries and wages	2.81	2.77	2.83	2.74
Books	1.1	0.93	0.84	0.74
Periodicals	0.92	0.84	0.76	0.82

Source: University Grants Committee. Statistics (Total Recurrent Expenditure excludes research grants and local rates)

siderable extent in protection of this their chief intellectual
capital asset. Along with this went a more realistic attitude
toward the soaring cost and multiplication of periodicals. Departments, which had once been urged to help by cutting down
on surplus journals and usually responded by eliminating all
those relevant to other departments, were now given specific
targets to meet. At York in 1982/83 it was decided to set aside
special funds for the library so that book purchase was raised
by 35 percent in money terms and we are doing the same in
1983/84. The second factor which had most effect in relaxing
the strain on purchase grants was the effectiveness of a generous premature retirement scheme that the government was
persuaded to finance. The result of this has been that in all
but the worst hit universities the savings from the retirement
of staff have exceeded the cuts and there has been a marked
improvement in their current cash flow. Of course, this has had
very serious academic consequences through the loss of large
numbers of academic staff and because of the random nature
of the retirement exercise. This has meant that staff have left
in a fashion that does not necessarily coincide with the requirements of rational academic planning, for to date there have
been no compulsory redundancies. But the consequence has
been to take the heat off the initial areas of cuts; buildings
are being maintained again, departmental and library grants
restored. The official library figures for 1982/83 are unavaila-
ble, but they will certainly show some relative decline in sal-

aries and wages, partly because of early retirement and partly because the ruling rate of salary increase, about 4 percent, is well below the level of inflation for books and periodicals. Preliminary figures from SCONUL, calculated in a different manner from those in Table 2.3, suggest that the median share of total spending on libraries as a share of recurrent grant in all U.K. universities rose from 4.1 percent in 1981/82 to 4.5 percent in 1982/83, and the median share of staff expenditure in library expenditure fell from 61.8 percent to 58.9 percent.

Of course, libraries have still in no way escaped from the cuts as we move into the third year of their operation but the burden of loss within the library system has been shifted. The process was under way before the end of 1981/82. The SCONUL survey showed libraries with around 60 academic related staff reporting losses of 2–4 posts and similar expectations as regards clerical posts. It all depended on the rate of vacancies. With early retirement and a general freeze on vacancies, 1982/83 was considerably worse in that respect. On the other hand, no library in 1982/83 reported getting less in sterling then in the previous year, and 40 were given at least partial compensation for inflation. But inflation looks likely to become the libraries' worst enemy again. The decline in sterling has already been mentioned. As the Blackwell survey for 1983 noted, most overseas suppliers had been paid before the pound began its big slide against the major currencies. The price of 1984 subscriptions to overseas journals will very much depend on what happens to the pound, which has not been doing too well. In addition, with general inflation well under control at around 4 percent, universities are being allowed only this amount as their cover against all increased costs. As Table 2.2 shows, U.K. periodicals rose by 11 percent between 1982 and 1983, books at probably no less a rate, and enquiries show no slackening currently.

The long-term prospects are not good. The government has already indicated that there are likely to be further regular reductions in funding during the rest of this decade quite apart from the great difficulties that will arise out of the sharp fall in student numbers expected after 1990. Computerization has certainly helped to reduce the number of staff required for day-to-day activities in libraries but apart from saving shelving space, most new technologies seem to be offering convenience rather than saving costs. The vicious circle in publishing referred to earlier will surely keep the prices of books and serials rising at a more rapid rate than the general rate of inflation if the present government is successful in its objectives in that regard, though there may be some relief if American interest rates fall and the dollar with them. Although the government has introduced a scheme to attract young academics into universities, it applies mostly to scientists and has little if anything to offer libraries. The problem is that the emphasis on technology and science may well make the situation of libraries still more difficult. Research grants in these areas bring money for consumables but rarely for scientific journals; academics working in the arts rarely bring in research money in any large amounts at all yet their need for library materials is no less important. The problem not often recognized is that one of the fundamental premises of university funding in Britain—the dual support system whereby the university recurrent grant is supposed to provide the backup for research as well as the means for teaching—has completely broken down through inadequacy of resources. One of the most serious consequences has been the declining ability of universities to make anything like adequate library provision for research materials.

At least one lesson must be taken on board by universities themselves. Now that they have warning of future cuts they must at least try logically to determine exactly what protection, if any, their libraries need rather than just let them take on the burden by chance as has happened over the last five years. After all perhaps the main question arising from Table 2.3 is not so much the shift between levels of expenditure discussed, but why the whole system let the library share sink so markedly. Librarians too must rethink their role. In these difficult economic circumstances should they, for example, be collecting or even retaining valuable, specialized volumes that rarely see the light of day and are even more rarely consulted? Is that not the role of national institutions? But how far should large university libraries come into this national category? Some librarians have used funds from windfall grants to buy expensive antiquarian items as an investment to be sold as and when necessary. Choices between staff, books, and serials will have to be the subject of long-term policy rather than of expediency. For all of us the future is not rosy and the least we can do is to learn the lessons of our latest bitter experience.

3

Financial Planning for Academic Librarians: Perceptions versus Realities

Edward R. Johnson

INTRODUCTION

In 1982 a questionnaire was sent to fifty-five directors of libraries at publicly-supported doctorate-granting universities.[1] Thirty-eight librarians responded. Of the 38 libraries represented, 31 were members of the Association of College and Research Libraries and seven were also members of the Association of Research Libraries. The average enrollment at the time of the 1982 study was similar to that of North Texas State University: 17,018 students. The responses to the questionnaire appear to be fairly representative of the problems and concerns of medium-sized academic libraries in the United States today.

Of particular interest to this paper on "perceptions versus hard realities" are the responses received in 1982 relating to budgeting and financial planning. Most of the respondents to the 1982 study predicted only moderate budget increases for their libraries during the next decade. Indeed, at best, many of them predicted relative stability; not decline, but not significant growth either. Fully two-thirds of the library directors surveyed concluded that the resources available to the library in the near future would not be sufficient to meet the teaching and research needs of their universities. This is an appalling finding but not a surprising one to anyone currently involved in academic administration.

Kay Jones recently reported on a similar questionnaire that she sent to 28 directors of academic libraries in the western United States. She found that only three reported no financial problems. Two-thirds of these librarians had experienced budget cuts or related problems in 1983.[2] I concluded in 1982, and Jones' findings support my conclusion, that academic libraries have entered a long period of genteel poverty. To be sure, many academic library administrators are looking for innovative alternatives and inaugurating formal planning processes to make their institutions more efficient and cost effective. Many are also, however, looking primarily to their institutional administrators for additional financial assistance to get them through these difficult years.

Despite the years of benign neglect suffered by academic librarians, documented by William Moffett,[3] the 1982 study revealed surprising optimism among library directors regarding the prospects of additional financial support from their institutions. The majority of respondents reported plans to seek additional funds beyond the regular library appropriation. In fact, they believed that supplemental funds from the university administration were just slightly less important than private donations to the financial future of their libraries.[4] Jones reported she was also surprised that "seventy-five percent of the university librarians . . . whose libraries have experienced financial restrictions in the past four years expressed the opinion that the cuts in book budget, reductions in staff, and other restrictions imposed were temporary in nature, although some defined 'temporary' as four to six years or longer!"[5]

The 1982 study concluded that academic library administrators seemed to be lowering their expectations somewhat and accepting the inevitability of increasing competition for funds among campus units. It also noted that " . . . the library is not in a particularly advantageous position competitively."[6] This disadvantage for most universities is due to the problems caused by insufficient resources for operating expenses and the large amounts of capital being invested in automation in all parts of the institution. Richard Talbot concluded that library finance is almost entirely dependent on institutional revenue and, since libraries have a settled place in the firmament of their institutions, they receive their "just" due and no more. Up to now, at least, it has not mattered whether or how library costs change or what new demands they are called upon to meet. On the whole, they still receive only their "fair share" of the institutional pie. The efforts of librarians to define library needs in ways that would enable them to obtain a greater fraction of the budget thus may seem irrelevant.[7]

THE REDUCTION OF ACADEMIC SUPPORT PROGRAMS

The optimism found by Jones and my study is all the more surprising when one considers that university administrators have been preventing financial collapse by whittling away at the "support" areas of the university's budget. They have been deferring building maintenance, "freezing" vacant clerical positions, cutting energy consumption, reducing the real compensation and fringe benefits of faculty and staff, and holding down library budgets. Indeed, university vice president Sigmund G. Ginsburg recently wrote that such decisions are, in fact, his institution's "clear-eyed and nonnostalgic" strategy for avoiding financial exigency.[8]

Mr. Ginsburg provided "ninety-nine ways to avoid financial exigency" in an article on that subject. Five of his suggestions, those relating to libraries, illustrate the perception gap that appears to exist between some academic librarians and university administrators over the financial realities of today:

38. "Emphasize interlibrary loans, use of technology, and other means of cost savings in order to reduce library expenses."

46. "Emphasize competitive bidding for goods and services. Explore with other institutions (educational and noneducational) the joint buying of goods and services in order to lower costs; explore with other educational institutions the sharing of library, transportation, maintenance, and instructional equipment . . . or arrange to minimize duplicating each others' programs, thus reducing expense."

56. "Postpone or defer major building refurbishment, new administrative or computer systems, or maintenance projects as long as possible (recognize that one cannot ignore these problems for too long)."

63. "Reduce expenditures for library equipment and materials. . . ."

68. "Reduce university subscriptions to newspapers, magazines, and journals."[9]

If Ginsburg's ideas are representative of many university administrators' attitudes toward the library, then academic librarians need to consider his suggestions in light of their own perceptions. In Ginsburg's article, for example, one finds no apparent support for the much-cherished notion that the center of the campus resides in the library. According to Robert M. O'Neil, the library, "like the heart in the human body . . . is the most vital organ in the academic community. . . ."[10] On the contrary, it appears that to some administrators the library is only one element of cost. It can be cut just like all of the other elements. The library, therefore, is entitled to no special exemption when things get tough financially in the view of some.

In Ginsburg's defense, his article is concerned only with how to stave off imminent financial disaster by immediate emergency short-term decisions. However, his article also illustrates, unintentionally, a major problem in academia today. Despite his claim that "a greater sense of trust, community, and involvement among all constituencies, particularly between faculty and administration, is to be fostered,"[11] one does not get the sense that the library's position would be very strong when retrenchments are made under his scheme.

Despite hundreds of mission statements, written goals, and objectives statements, it is evident that universities still have a long way to go in terms of establishing reasonable priorities, setting realistic goals, and developing logical plans to achieve those goals. Ginsburg, for instance, does not discuss the possible long-range impact of his recommendations on individual units. His suggestions do not address the crucial question of reviewing or eliminating weak or redundant academic programs which, surely, is the very core of the problem facing most institutions of higher learning. Ginsburg notes, almost as an aside, that such actions are "important."[12] Responding as a librarian to Ginsburg's 99 suggestions I believe that by cutting a little here and a little there, the university may ultimately be wounding itself permanently.

GOALS AND OBJECTIVES RELATING TO
ACADEMIC SUPPORT UNITS

Universities of late have been feverishly writing mission statements and defining institutional goals and objectives as part of an intensified national interest in formal planning programs. More and more institutions of higher education are employing modern management techniques to improve their operational effectiveness. The experts are telling university administrators that they have to be innovative and willing to take risks, to develop strategies, and to establish priorities.

Despite all this activity, however, it still seems to be the general pattern for universities to make across-the-board reductions, thereby weakening nearly all academic and, especially, support units and programs. A few institutions have made well-publicized efforts to reduce or eliminate weak academic programs. They are in the minority. My experience at two universities is that the more common approach to planning is to deal with short-term problems first and to delay, sometimes indefinitely, the long-range ones. The "academic support" units' budgets in some places have been reduced to near-emergency levels of weakness. Rosabeth M. Kanter observed that planning often seems to follow, rather than to precede, decision-making. "Some analysts," she noted, "even say that organizations formulate strategy *after* they implement it."[13]

THE LIBRARY AS THE HEART OF THE
UNIVERSITY

Many university presidents undoubtedly agree with their colleague O'Neil who has stated that the library

is the center of research and a key to the university's scholarly distinction. It is a mounting and at times uncontrollable drain on the university's budget. It is a window to the community—both the academic community and the general citizenry. It is the most dependable link with other institutions of higher learning. It can be an administrative headache and at times a battleground of personnel policies. It is the source of greatest promise and greatest problems in the use of new technologies. It is the key to development of new academic programs and the strength of existing programs.[14]

Despite such somewhat mixed expressions of support, there is a striking lack of identification of library problems, needs, and plans in most university statements of goals and objectives. Libraries, if included at all in such statements, are frequently given only brief and passing mention. My own institution, for example, recently produced a university-wide statement of mission and goals and objectives. The library section, as is often the case, is mostly mixed in with general goals for all academic support units. There is one goal specific to the library. "The University," it states, "should continue efforts to increase state appropriations for the libraries and to supplement those funds through support groups and external contributions."[15] This is a worthy goal, to be sure, but one that is too general to be very useful in planning.

If O'Neil is correct that the library is the "key to the university's scholarly distinction" then how do we account for the widespread lack of useful consideration of library problems in institutional plans? The reason for such a notable lack can be found in the perceptions of many academic administrators regarding the library. There is a problem with separating reality from rhetoric. The reality is that many administrators either do not take the library's problems seriously enough or choose to ignore them.

Rather than being central to university plans and aspirations, then, the library is often taken for granted or ignored. The cliche that what is everybody's business is also no one's business applies, tragically, to most academic libraries. The result is what Richard Talbot characterized as "an excruciating dilemma." He found that "the percentage of the budget provided to libraries is unlikely to be increased because there is a ceiling, no matter how ill-defined, beyond which institutions will not go in supporting their libraries, since to do so would subvert other institutional purposes."[16] Today, academic libraries receive pretty much the same percentage of the institutional budget that they did a decade or two ago, new programs, inflation, and other problems notwithstanding. Instead of being the "most vital organ in the academic community," the library is really on the fringe of that community in regard to resource allocation and decision-making.

George Keller's recent book *Academic Strategy* noted that many universities still rely on "incrementalism" rather than strategic planning in making decisions for the future.[17] In such an environment, politics, rumor, competition, bargaining, and personal persuasion are the major influential factors in determining priorities. The library is usually at a disadvantage in such an environment.

The library administrator does not have a group of prominent alumni whom he can call upon for support. The library can not cite the pressure of enrollment as powerfully and persuasively as can, for example, the college of business or the department of computer science. As an academic support unit, the library is highly dependent upon administrative and faculty understanding and acceptance. But, lacking political clout, in the competition for scarce resources in an incrementalist environment, the library often receives more moral than financial support.

SUGGESTIONS FOR ACADEMIC ADMINISTRATORS

1. The most important suggestion to academic administrators for improving the library is to involve library administrators more closely in the institutional decision-making process. Although the librarian is, indeed, a central person on campus, able to see the institution as a whole, he or she is seldom consulted about university-wide decisions. Moffett found this lack of involvement to be a major concern of academic library administrators around the country.[18] Keller strongly recommended that " . . . politically most of the key people need to be on board the strategy train when it leaves the station. Participation is imperative."[19] Robert M. Rosenzweig, in an analysis of research universities, concurred that the inclusion of librarians in policy-making is crucial to the future of universities.[20]

2. The goals and objectives of the library need to be more

carefully considered and understood by the top administration. Library goals and objectives should be included in overall institutional plans. Library problems should not be ignored because they are difficult to solve. Ralph Ellsworth said many years ago that "the moment libraries cease to be problems to university presidents, the time will have arrived when humanistic scholarship is dead."[21] Realistic strategic planning must be based on a better understanding of the library's role in the university.

3. Improved and more open communications are vital to successful academic planning. Lack of sufficient information can hamper otherwise well-laid plans. But virtually every university or college librarian in the country can recount tale after tale of academic programs begun or ended without any consultation whatsoever concerning library resources. The library may represent only four, five, or six percent of a university's budget but that is a significant percentage; too significant to be overlooked so routinely. It seems that just about the only time the library budget is considered important is when the need arises to make cutbacks. University administrators need to get to know their library better, to talk to its staff, to spend some time behind the scenes, and to find out what its problems and needs are. Too often, decisions are made at the top level based on scanty information or, worse, on superficial impressions.

4. As noted earlier, Ginsburg urged interinstitutional cooperation as a library tactic to avoid financial exigency. He does not need to persuade many academic librarians with the logic of this goal. He needs to convince his administrative colleagues. A problem common to many cooperative library programs is insufficient understanding and lack of true support at the upper levels of university administration. Librarians cannot make such programs succeed by themselves. Significant institutional commitment, of financial and other resources, is required for these cooperative programs to succeed. The saving of money may not be an immediate result but the programs will thereby be strengthened.

5. It is time to reconsider the practice of providing the library with only its "fair share" of the resources. As Talbot ob-

served, it can hardly be a coincidence that in good times or bad, the library's percentage of the institutional budget remains about the same. If the library is, in fact, the key to new academic programs and the strength of existing programs, then it should be supported accordingly.

SUGGESTIONS FOR LIBRARY ADMINISTRATORS

1. "Strategy making," according to Keller, "is a blend of rational and economic analysis, political maneuvering, and psychological interplay. It is therefore participatory. . . . "[22] In other words, library administrators need to jump into the political arena even if they are not invited. Leadership requires action rather than mere reaction. Sound financial and strategic library planning requires considerable political acumen on the part of the library administrator. Above all, it is imperative that the library become more closely involved in university-wide decision-making, convincing university administrators that librarians have skills and insights that need to be exploited.

2. There seems to be a growing use of planning techniques by academic library administrators. Realistic and attainable goals need to be set so that library priorities can be agreed upon with university administrators. Just as vague, high-sounding mission statements do not lead to concrete accomplishments for the university, neither do fuzzy or unrealistic goals lead to results for the library. Thoughtful and imaginative goals and objectives are an excellent medium to improve communications between the library and the university administration.

3. Fund-raising is no longer an endeavor to be left to some central office in the university. University administrators are expecting library directors to concentrate on fund-raising from external sources, not internal ones. Such fund-raising requires intensive effort and often produces modest results for libraries. But, during the next decade, many academic libraries face inevitable decline if they depend solely on the state

legislature or their institution's already overextended budgets.

4. University administrators must give real support to interinstitutional cooperation. Library directors must also continue their efforts in this direction. Cooperative collection development, bibliographic access, preservation and conservation, and use of new technology will, in many parts of the country, mean the difference between mere survival and excellence for participating libraries.

5. The subtitle of this paper is "perceptions versus hard realities." Academic library administrators need to reevaluate their perceptions in light of the hard economic realities of the 1980s. Librarians need to be better informed about university-wide problems and concerns. University presidents and vice presidents view libraries as bottomless pits for money. Today, more than ever, they are forced to choose between such things as repairing leaky roofs or supplementing the library's periodical budget. Often, of course, they cannot do both.

Patience on the librarian's part and support for university priorities may sometimes be needed instead of mere requests for extra funds. Many librarians may, indeed, be able to persuade institutions to supplement the library's budget. But many others need to be more realistic about the prospects of additional financial assistance from universities. Merely stating that the library should be one of the highest university priorities will not make it happen. Library administrators need to demonstrate: first, that they are making wise use of the resources allocated to them, and second, that improved support of the library benefits everyone in the university—administration, faculty, and students alike regardless of position or discipline.

NOTES

1. Edward R. Johnson, "Financial Planning Needs of Publicly-Supported Academic Libraries in the 1980s: Politics as Usual," *Journal of Library Administration* 3 (Fall/Winter 1982), 23–26.

2. Kay Jones, "Financial Restrictions in Academic Libraries," *College and Research Libraries News* 44 (September 1983), 269–270.

3. William A. Moffett, "Don't Shelve Your College Librarian," *Educational Record* 63 (Summer 1982), 46–50.

4. Johnson, "Financial Planning Needs," 26.

5. Jones, "Financial Restrictions in Academic Libraries," 269.

6. Johnson, "Financial Planning Needs," 33.

7. Richard J. Talbot, "Financing the Academic Library," in Thomas J. Galvin and Beverly P. Lynch, eds., *Priorities for Academic Libraries* (San Francisco: Jossey-Bass, 1982), 36, 39–40.

8. Sigmund G. Ginsburg, "Avoiding Financial Exigency," *Educational Record* 64 (Summer 1983), 40–46.

9. Ibid., 45–46.

10. Robert M. O'Neil, "The University Administrator's View of the University Library," in Galvin and Lynch, eds., *Priorities for Academic Libraries*, 5.

11. Ginsburg, "Avoiding Financial Exigency," 46.

12. Ibid.

13. Rosabeth Moss Kanter, "Change Masters and the Intricate Structure of Corporate Culture Change," *Management Review* 72 (October 1983), 20.

14. O'Neil, "The University Administrator's View," 5.

15. *The Mission of North Texas State University (1983)* (Denton, Texas: North Texas State University, September, 1983), 5.

16. Talbot, "Financing the Academic Library," 39–40.

17. George Keller, *Academic Strategy: The Management Revolution in American Higher Education* (Baltimore: Johns Hopkins University Press, 1983), 106–113.

18. Moffett, "Don't Shelve Your College Librarian."

19. Keller, *Academic Strategy*, 149.

20. Robert M. Rosenzweig, *The Research Universities and Their Patrons* (Berkeley: University of California Press, 1982), 82.

21. Ralph E. Ellsworth, "Libraries, Students, and Faculty," in *The Cornell Library Conference: Papers Presented at the Dedication of the Central Library, October, 1962* (Ithaca, N.Y.: Cornell University Library, 1964), 81.

22. Keller, *Academic Strategy*, 149.

II

CHANGING APPROACHES

4

Supporting Scholarship in Universities: A Response to the Growing Cost of Information Services

Maurice Glicksman

In research universities the priority given to libraries in the allocation of scarce university funds is very high. Support for the major scholarly resource for many faculty and students is widespread among faculty, and almost as strong among students. During the past decade, libraries have done well in the competition for funds. At Brown University, our advisory committee on the budget considers more than twenty different important functions and concludes that the top three priorities include the libraries. After reviewing budgetary allocations elsewhere, I believe that this is also true at many other institutions.

If this is the case, we might well ask why there is concern among administrators and librarians about the inadequacy of library support, and about the deterioration of library collections. Both of these perceptions are real: the number of volumes added annually to collections decreased from 1976 to 1982 and increased only in 1983,[1] and the allocation of funds to preserve the collections held and needed for future scholars is far short of the minimum necessary.[2] The reason for the problem is evident. The cost of purchasing books, serials, microforms, and similar materials and of providing the needed library services has risen more rapidly than has the income to universities, the general higher education price index, the consumer price index, or the standard of living index![3] Although universities have allocated an increasing share of their income to libraries, they have not been able to maintain momentum in keeping up with new scholarship, nor to attack the long-growing deficit in preserving properly the materials they have held for some time.

One major contributor to the inflation in costs is the growth in number and price of serials. There has been a proliferation of serial publication in almost every discipline and an inflation of the price of books and serials which has been extraordinarily high. Because of the disparity between the growth of personal income and library funds, and the inflation in serial costs, an increasing number of higher-priced journals has meant some decrease in the average number of subscriptions. Publishers increase the price to compensate for falling circulation, which leads to further falling circulation, which leads to increased prices, and so on. The normal operations of the free market would probably have stopped this spiral some time ago if research libraries were not providing increased funding to keep so many of the journals operating.

Administrative support for the libraries has reflected the priorities of the faculty and students. During the 1976–82 period, 90 universities belonging to the Association of Research Libraries increased their library expenditures at a rate of over 12.7 percent per year, while salaries and wages and the higher education price index were each increasing at rates of about 8.5 percent per year.[1] About 40 percent of the university members of the Association of Research Libraries allocated 4 percent or more of their education and general budgets to their libraries in 1982/83, and five universities used at least 7 percent of their budgets that year for their libraries.[4]

An increase in the commitment of university resources cannot continue indefinitely. The challenge university administrators and librarians now face is how to maintain and enhance the vital support provided by the libraries in the light of the limitations on available resources. We face the need for increasing funds for the acquisition of additional materials, for the services to make those materials useful, and for the preservation of the materials held. We face the need for new funds to improve access to and use of the libraries' holdings with the assistance of advanced computer and communication systems. We also face the need for additional space for the expanded holdings of recent years, and for the new kinds of equipment required by libraries as a result of the changing modes of communication and storage of information.

There are practical responses to the opportunities presented by the need for greater resources. These responses call for cooperation, coordination, a willingness to give up some autonomy in return for increased scholarly capital, and a hard-nosed but open approach to the use of technology.

RESOURCE SHARING

Universities have held tenaciously to the conviction that the results of scholarly investigation should be made available to all who have a need to make use of it, or who wish to be informed about it. Access for scholars to scholarly work is especially to be supported and enhanced. Adherence to such a principle has provided an important positive impetus to the constructive growth of the scholarly community, and to the real advance in understanding which has helped our society to develop its strengths.

To achieve this goal requires that the results of scholarly work be made broadly available. This means that information about what has been "written" should also be made broadly available. Publication in journals, monographs, informal papers, books, and on-line text are all means to this end. Bibliographic data for all of these forms of publication are essential to their use. Broad availability of bibliographic records is hence also vital to the maintenance of the scholarly enterprise.

There is presently no single place where scholars can go and be assured that they have access to all of the documents and information necessary for their work. There is presently no one place where there is even a collection of guides describing the location of all that might be available to assist scholars in scholarly work. And as time goes on, any one place *by itself* will fail by a larger margin to accomplish this task.

The scholarly community has adjusted to these realities.

Scholars try to collect as much as possible of what they need, in their own institution if not in their personal libraries. They engage in informal contacts with colleagues to exchange information. They travel to known aggregations of material important for their work, or they borrow the material needed. Libraries play an integral role in this sharing process through the interlibrary loan system. For more recent books and journals there are collections of limited bibliographic data—in regularly issued printed volumes, or provided by various abstract services in printed form, or accessible through computer terminals in an on-line mode. Scholarly societies collect and publish descriptions of currently published materials, and private businesses also provide such a service, at a price which is demonstrably profitable.

The involvement of research libraries (or the parent universities) in attempts to accommodate to the realities is informal: there are few formal and truly cooperative ventures that have been developed by research libraries. The association of academic groups for the purpose of satisfying some need not well-addressed by the individual members is a well-known phenomenon. It occurs in athletics (the NCAA, the Big Ten, and the Ivy League are examples); it occurs in research (the Universities Research Association and the National Radio Astronomy Observatory); it is present in research libraries (the Association of Research Libraries, the Center for Research Libraries, and the Research Libraries Group); it occurs in scholarly publishing (the University Press of New England); it is present in many scholarly disciplines and even between disciplines (the Modern Languages Association and the American Council of Learned Societies, and the American Association of Engineering Societies). But almost all of these are marked by very limited responsibilities taken on by the cooperating groups, and hence very limited *sharing* of responsibilities of the institutions with the consortial group. We keep the consortium on a short string as much as possible. The controversy over the governance and activities of the NCAA exemplifies the problems which can arise when institutions find that the consortial activities or actions do not fit well into their own sets of values or goals. The institution can try to convince the consortium to modify its approach, or it can withdraw, if the price of so doing is affordable.

What are the compelling reasons for institutions to join in cooperative ventures in resource sharing, whether the resources are mainly their own or provided by outside agencies (including foundations, governments, industry, and private donors)? There are a number of factors which play important roles.

Size

A new venture of interest to several institutions may be seen as too large and even inappropriate for a single institution to sponsor. This may be because the initial and/or ultimate scales are of size comparable to that of several of the institutions involved; it may also be because the goals of the new enterprise are compatible with but not central to those of individual institutions. Some universities do sponsor very large operations (the Lincoln Laboratory of the Massachusetts Institute of Technology, the Forrestal Center of Princeton University, and the Jet Propulsion Laboratory of the California Institute of Technology for example), but then take care to insulate these large research and development organizations so that they do not intrude heavily on the basic mission of the institution. Even this attempt at insulation may not avoid questions of identity and identification (for example, MIT with the Draper Laboratory, and the University of California with the Livermore Laboratory). And most of these organizations are really "resource-sharing" in that they are operated for the benefit of the whole community and are open to use by scholars at other institutions who need to make use of the facilities. The principle of open and broad availability of scholarly resources is maintained. But policy decisions are the responsibility of the governing institution, subject to review by the supporting agency.

In many of the cases where these large organizations are operated by a single institution this is a result of historical development. Usually a faculty member at the institution provided the leadership, and the project started out at a modest level, without a commitment to a large-scale organization in the early phases. As the project developed, the individuals interested in it clustered at the institution under the leader, and success led eventually to large size.

We should be careful to note a factor important to universities. All of the large enterprises run by single institutions receive the bulk of their financial support from outside agencies. The discomfort to the institution when this support is withdrawn is real, but accepted (one example of such is the Princeton-Penn Accelerator), and the organization is allowed to disappear or reduce its size to a supportable level. Institutions are thus properly cautious about the level and duration of the *institutional* commitment they make. In the case of ventures housed and controlled by the single institution, there is no evident threat to the autonomy of the institution itself.

Complementarity of Strengths and Interests

Institutions see that they have current strengths which can be more effectively used if they are put together in cooperation with complementary strengths present at other institutions. These can occur in a number of fields. Some institutions have joint academic programs with another institution: cross-registration of courses, for example, is not uncommon for institutions in close proximity to each other. Others may share supporting services (security and energy sources, among others). Bilateral and consortial arrangements involving universities and colleges in different countries are increasing in number, and are good examples of this sharing by faculty and by students of complementary institutional strengths. A number of universities and research centers arrange for the sharing of faculty. Institutions also share graduate students: these students benefit from the availability of a particular expertise or facility which is important but not central to the student's educational and research program.

It should be clear that the maximum advantage which can be gained from such arrangements occurs when institutions are willing to give up something in return for the values to be received from the cooperation. Obviously, the desire to duplicate the complementing service or function at the other institution(s) should be resisted. To gain maximum value from the cooperation, the institutions involved may have to invest in joint resources they might otherwise not support individually.

Cooperation to Achieve "Critical Mass"

Institutions may have important programs which are too small to be viable. They either cost too much for the benefits received by the institution, or need to involve more people for intellectual strength and vitality. Examples of this exist in the field of scholarly publishing and in areas of research collaboration requiring major facilities. In many cases the choice is between terminating valuable programs or developing cooperative ventures.

Here it is also important that the cooperating institutions recognize the investment they will make in the cooperative venture. It is truly a collaboration in this case, with the acceptance of varying roles by each participant. Institutions may have to accept some constraints on their own freedom of action for the "good of the whole."

SUCCESSFUL EXAMPLES OF COOPERATION

The following are examples of cooperative ventures which can be described in terms of the above factors. Choices outside of the library field are arbitrary and are made because of the author's familiarity and not because of uniqueness.

Universities Research Association

The Universities Research Association (URA) operates a high energy physics research facility, the Fermilab in Illinois, with support from the Department of Energy. This arrangement developed out of proposals by members of the community of high energy research physicists for a major facility to provide for exploration of phenomena occurring at particle energies higher than available at other facilities at that time. Scholars agreed on the kind of facility needed. Interested institutions agreed to form a management organization and allow an open search for a site for the facility. The governmental agency providing financial support guided the process.

Control of policy is in the hands of a board of directors elected by a council of presidents; each of the 54 university members has its chief executive officer as a member of the governing council, which meets annually. Operational control is in the hands of the Fermilab director, who is responsible to the board.

But this organization receives very minor financial support from the university members, and the operational and capital costs are supported by the federal government, in response to detailed proposals made by URA to the Department of Energy. Its annual budget is comparable to or even larger than the budgets of many of URA's member institutions. URA is an example where the size factor may have been the dominant one, but complementarity and critical mass also played roles. Almost all research projects undertaken at Fermilab involve large groups of physicists from several institutions. There is no requirement that the participating scientists have to be affiliated with one of the member institutions.

Research Libraries Group

This example evolved in a different way. A new venture was developed by an institution, and was then seen as a bit too ambitious in scope and cost for one institution alone. This seems to have been the case with the BALLOTS system developed by Stanford University for bibliographic record storage and searching. Alternatives to termination would have been to market it as a product, and hence to seek to develop a financial support level among users, or to engage other institutions with similar goals in a cooperative venture using what had been developed as the base. Similar choices have faced a number of institutions which have developed technological products useful in libraries. Stanford eventually followed the second route. The result was a merger with or absorption into the Research Libraries Group (RLG), a cooperative of four libraries which had been seeking to develop an appropriate system for the production of easily accessible and searchable bibliographic records. An increased membership would involve major research libraries in a cooperative venture to provide quality services at an acceptable cost, and to engage in research and development of a set of initiatives which would assist the institutions in resource sharing. Members of RLG name representatives to a governing board, which determines policy for the organization. Present membership includes 26 institutions. Present policy provides that many of the services are available only to members.

RLG provides an example of the operation of the factors of size and critical mass (of resources, primarily). Funding which supports RLG has come from member institutions and from foundations. Hence there has been a commitment of resources by the member institutions to assure continuing viability of the organization. Funds which might otherwise have been used in other library operations in-house are being used to support the cooperative venture. There is some apparent reduction in institutional autonomy, since policy decisions made by the board do not require unanimity of support by the institutions, and the services provided and planned are key elements of current library operations. However, peer pressure rather than rigid regulation has been used in order to convince member institutions to provide major financial support. Of course, members may withdraw if there is major disagreement with the policy and direction of the cooperative enterprise, but they would do so with some resultant deterioration in library services.

University Press of New England

The support of scholarly publication is seen as a desirable contribution to the scholarly enterprise by faculty at many research universities: the Association of American University Presses numbers 74 members. However, most of these presses neither operate on a sufficient scale nor follow a policy aggressively profit-oriented in their choice of books published to avoid unprofitable operation, requiring substantial annual subsidies from the institutional budgets as well as subventions from some of the authors.

Association with the University Press of New England

(UPNE) was entered into by its eight member institutions in major part because they concluded that it was uneconomical for them to operate individual, independent presses. None of them expects to end up with a financial profit on their cooperative venture, but they will end up with much more value for their investment in scholarly publishing.

UPNE involves both cooperation and collaboration. When one of the member institutions wishes to publish a book, the cooperative mode is involved. Once the project is endorsed by the institution, it must then be accepted by the editorial board of UPNE. It is then published by UPNE for the member press (for example, "by UPNE for the Brown University Press"). The member guarantees the financial investment. The UPNE staff provides the needed editorial and production services more economically than in the case of the member institution on its own. The collaborative mode operates when the UPNE editor and the editorial board accept manuscripts to be published under consortium (UPNE) sponsorship alone. These are then financed out of consortial funds, which come from membership dues, foundations, and any retained profits.

UPNE is an example of the critical mass factor in operation. Its governance structure is simple: a governing board of representatives selected by the member institutions, and an editorial board similarly constituted. The governing board deals with policy issues (including the selection and evaluation of the performance of the director/editor of UPNE) and the editorial board deals with the merit of proposed publications.

The Center for Research Libraries

Almost forty years ago a number of midwestern universities agreed to establish a new organization which would serve as a repository for parts of their collections which saw little use in any one institution. Duplication would be eliminated, and the pressure for providing increased space for growing collections would be eased. They obtained financial support from foundations for the initial capital investment, engaged a director, and started what is now the Center for Research Libraries (CRL). This organization has expanded in size (more than 100 members) and purchases as well as receives material (now over 3,500,000 items) which it holds for the use of its members and others. Its purpose is to be a supplemental library for its library members: a library whose holdings complement and supplement the holdings of its member libraries, a library that provides efficient access to its holdings to the scholars who require them.

Its initial membership of 10 or 11 institutions has increased steadily, but the growth was enhanced during the past decade as CRL expanded the services it offered, including copies of journal articles from the British Lending Library Division when its own holdings did not include the requested items. And there was some pressure from some members for CRL to undertake some of the goals of the national periodicals center[2, 5] which had been proposed earlier but not funded by the Congress. In the past two years, CRL members have had the opportunity to debate questions of policy and direction, and have determined to restrict the mission of the cooperative venture to its "traditional" role of acquiring, holding, and making available uncommon scholarly materials which complement and supplement the holdings of its member institutions. CRL provides for efficiency through the elimination of unneeded duplication, hence saving its members the cost of acquiring, holding, and storing/preserving material. It has recently enlarged its space as part of a long-range program to provide adequate quarters for its expanding holdings. Its services are available to nonmembers on an "occasional use" basis.

Governance of CRL involves a council on which all regular members are represented, and a board of directors which is elected by the council. The council meets annually; the board meets three or four times a year, and is responsible for overseeing the operations, including the choice and evaluation of the performance of the director. The council deals with general policy and approves the annual budget.

CRL seems to fit best into the category of complementarity of strengths and interests. Its members share an interest in seeing that its holdings and services complement their own; they must also recognize that they obtain maximum benefit from their involvement in CRL when they tailor their own policies to mesh with those of CRL. Doing this requires cooperation and interest in, knowledge of and acceptance of mutual goals; it also means some decrease in individual institutional autonomy.

FUTURE NEEDS OF THE RESEARCH LIBRARY WORLD

There are three major challenges for libraries which I believe must be met in the coming decades:

— how to deal efficiently with the growing quantity of scholarly material;
— how to respond to the deteriorating quality of the form of materials held; and
— how to guide the introduction of new technology to maximize utility and minimize cost.

Each of these calls for cooperation and collaboration among research libraries, but it would be a mistake for the community to decide that one organization can provide all of the solutions. In fact, a considerable number of cooperating ventures will be involved, some not yet in existence. There will also have to be some kind of guidance—more than the minimum expectation of good communication among the libraries—provided in a form accepted by the community, and thus ensuring maximum participation, optimum quality of enterprise, and the greatest usefulness of the results.

Growing Quantity of Material

The quantity of materials necessary for continuing scholarship increases with time. The materials exist in different forms: uncoded contrasting visual patterns on various material substances (for example, books and serials, manuscripts, musical and dance scores, photographs, art, microforms), and coded patterns stored on and in various material substances (for example, musical records, videodisks, magnetic tape and disks, electronic "chips"). They have to be acquired, held in quarters secure against deterioration or injury, and "recorded" so that scholars may learn about their existence and contents, and find them with a minimum of effort.

The challenge faced has two parts: the need to know about the material available (its content and location), and the need to obtain and hold the material securely for maximum utility to the scholarly community.

A form of common bibliographic description and assured access to that description are required. The need for the production and storage of retrievable records is being addressed by at least three major institutions: the Library of Congress, OCLC, Inc., and the Research Libraries Group. Each organization is of a different nature and serves somewhat different functions. The Library of Congress has played a key role in obtaining agreement on a common form for the records, in addition to providing a large data base for many scholarly materials. OCLC, a private service organization which also engages in research, and RLG, a cooperative nonprofit service and research organization, have been developing large data bases for their members, accessible through electronic means as well as in the still common standard of old: the catalog card.

As these efforts continue, they should lead to the realization of our goal: the quick and economical availability to scholars of bibliographic information on the holdings available in all libraries. Cooperation among the large data-base holders is essential to the achievement of this goal. OCLC and RLG store the records of materials held by their members, and the individual libraries have records of their own holdings, as well as access to information about what is held at other libraries. Communication among the libraries and large data bases is steadily being improved.

The present trend points to the emergence of an organization of networks which may have to be managed by a new cooperative utility. In neighborhood areas (such as the northeast, the northwest, the southwest, the mountain states, and the southeast) there would be medium-size data bases, containing perhaps tens of millions of records, linked by a communications net to individual libraries with their million(s) of records of local holdings. The "neighborhood" base could be linked to one or several major data storage facilities, with comprehensive national and international holdings. Scholars would have on-line access to the records at the local library; when they failed to find the record sought, or wished to search more broadly for related material, they would be led to the neighborhood utility base, and ultimately to one or more of the national stores.

What is required is an organization and an adequate method of dealing with the costs of such an arrangement. RLG already has long-range plans for encouraging arrangements similar to the simple one described above. Whether such will be managed by RLG for the community, or by a new cooperative utility or series of such utilities independent of RLG cannot be predicted now. The existence of such a set of networks will also await the economic and technical environment which can make them possible. However, the base for such a future utility is already being shaped, in the growing collection of electronically accessible bibliographic records, and the growing number of libraries which are making electronic searching of these data bases broadly available to the scholarly community.

A knottier problem is the increasing quantity of material itself. The national periodicals center[2,5] was envisaged as one solution to the problem, but it appears that federal funding for such a venture is not in the offing in the near future. If we look at what was planned, perhaps it is possible to see a way out for our libraries.

It is well understood[2] that scholars will continue to expect immediate access to journals and books to which they will frequently refer. Many journals presently purchased by research libraries fall into this group, but there are also many which do not and which are rarely used. Such "uncommon" material is a natural subject for cooperative "collecting." Because an individual scholar may look for it very rarely, the absence from the library is acceptable; but inability to locate it promptly for the scholar is deemed undesirable. Hence such material should be stored in a location which provides rapid response to a request for the material, and which also identifies its ownership of the material to all libraries which might have a need for it.

There are two obvious ways of responding to the situation. One is to use the interlibrary loan system, much enhanced in usefulness by the presence of the network of bibliographic services described above. In order to assist in the costs of communications and of the transfer of items, and to handle the increasing serials costs, it is desirable to couple this with individual libraries agreeing to limit their acquisition and holdings of such uncommon materials. One example would be to have the "neighborhood" utility manager also be a collaborative collection developer: libraries in the neighborhood would agree to continue to acquire certain items, and drop others, as long as the whole group had access to the necessary and desirable uncommon material. Communication links could obviate the need for a central collection in the neighborhood.

Another approach would be to have a central location, or several locations geographically distributed, in which uncommon material would be stored. The Center for Research Libraries already provides such a service for some limited classes of materials. It could embrace such an ambitious function, or help to nucleate possible new cooperating groups to provide such a service. In its current development of collection policy directions, CRL has taken modest steps in this direction.

Emphasis on serials and books published abroad and in foreign languages will serve to provide minimum disruption to the economics of publication. Nevertheless, if such a program is to succeed, it will lead to a decrease in the number of subscriptions. Unless the North American libraries market is a small part of the publishers' market, the economies envisaged will be limited if the publications are to continue.

The alternative organizational scenarios are both possible; the first is organizationally more complex, since responsibility for the holding of materials and the delivery of service is shared rather than concentrated. With centers holding serials and other materials, the supporting members of the cooperative center can assure efficiency, develop the center policies, and shape its future directions. They can decide to cancel their own subscriptions, but need not if they wish to provide redundancy for their own good reasons. In the case where the linkage is only one of communications, the institution needing service does not and probably should not determine the policies of the other libraries which provide the material desired. Peer pressure for cooperation would be the important force. The major distinction between the two approaches is the implication of greater restrictions in individual autonomy apparent in the first. It also requires the implementation of good bibliographic networking. And it would require an agreement among libraries as to how to apportion the costs, again involving some restriction on individual institutional autonomy much greater than appears to have been acceptable in the past.

The development of centers for holding uncommon materials, whether part of the Center for Research Libraries or a new cooperative, provides the best response to the challenge. These centers would be libraries of libraries, jointly owned and accepted as such. (The apparent lack of perception of this ownership by some of its members is one of the current concerns in CRL which has to be overcome.) Joint ownership means the investment of common funds, given or raised by the members, in the space for the material held, as well as the materials themselves. Management of the centers should serve its owners, but in an enlightened manner. The goals of the cooperative have to be recognized as goals of a group, and not of any particular individual in that group; some subservience of the interests of its individual owners to the greater interests of the centers has to be not only accepted but also championed.

As cooperation evolves, it may eventually be most effective to have the "neighborhood" storage utility hold bibliographic information not only of the collections of its neighborhood members, but also of the uncommon materials held jointly for them. A possible scenario for the future, in which much of the new journal material is distributed electronically and stored on disks (magnetic, video, or other), would enhance the possibility of such a merger of the two functions.

Preservation

No librarian advocates the preservation of every item held in every library. The cost is too great. This challenge seems to be on its way to being addressed, provided funds can become available in sufficient quantity to do the job.

What is the job? There are two parts: preservation of substance and preservation of content. For unique materials of scholarly interest, libraries have been taking care of the problem as best they can. These materials are primarily in rare book libraries, where attention is paid to preservation of the underlying substance, and copies of the material are produced for use by those scholars who require only the content of the material. The Library of Congress has been a leader in studying the technology as it is developing, and RLG has recently played a key role in obtaining foundation support for the copying of some of the highest priority material to provide master copies available to future scholars. This approach should be supported and expanded.

A key element in meeting this challenge is the decision to duplicate only one copy of a given item. This requires cooperation through central management of the funding and of an open competition among institutions for the categories of material to be copied. It also requires agreement that the copies produced be available to all scholars needing them. The leadership taken by the RLG in this process is to be commended and supported. As RLG's involvement continues, it may find that it is also becoming a library, as a result of its holding of the master copies of material being "preserved."

New Technology

Reference to new technology pervades the library scene today. Computers are used by many libraries to keep track of their orders and of the circulation of their collections. Computers are being used to store and organize the search of large bibliographic data bases. Research on preservation and on the use of high-density magnetic, optical, and electronic media for the storage of information is being actively pursued in the library community as well as outside it.

The future use of this technology, in the library field as in other areas of our society, will most likely be very great. Its future form cannot be predicted accurately today. The broad distribution of computers, particularly in the homes of many people in our society, can have a profound effect on libraries. Sufficient attention has not been paid to the communication "protocol" for this rapidly growing family of devices. But there is bound to be a demand for an economical and efficient means of access to library holdings by people using computers. Even more important to the research libraries is the commitment being made to distribute computer work stations very broadly to students and faculty at many colleges and universities.

The rapid development of appropriate technology is forcing institutions to consider expanding its use in the libraries. Attention is being drawn to computer systems which can provide machine-accessible records (such as, on-line catalogue, ordering information, and circulation information) which can be economically produced and easily searched. What has not occurred as yet, however, is a cooperative approach to developing standards for the computer software used in handling the electronic record and accessing it, so as to enhance rather than impede broad availability.

Librarians should be concerned that the community of libraries, particularly research libraries, is currently dependent on the many developers and manufacturers of diverse computer systems for the libraries. It is worth noting that the general society has had to deal with the fact that IBM, Digital, Data General, Hewlett Packard, Wang, Apple, and others use different operating systems in their computers, and that the transfer of information between the products of different manufacturers is difficult, to say the least. An obvious advantage to the manufacturers when compact systems were being sold, this lack of compatibility is now being accepted as a handicap in the developing field of linked computers. Hence there are reports of moves by several manufacturers to encourage some commonality or at least greater ease of translation from one manufacturer's machines to those of another.

If libraries introduce diverse systems, particularly catalogue systems, into their libraries, the vision of networks of communication links among libraries will be more difficult to fulfill. Before a library will be able to link its system with those of its colleagues, it will have to provide for appropriate code translation. It is important for libraries to make every effort to impress on the manufacturers and developers of systems that compatibility of linkage with diverse systems is a priority. This is a clear example where it will be worthwhile for individual libraries to think of the needs of the whole community, and to be willing to sacrifice some measure of what they feel they need for their own library to achieve a more useful community system.

No group has yet seen this as a sufficiently important problem to seek to address. The Association of Research Libraries and the Council on Library Resources should study the situation to confirm the possible magnitude of the problem and develop some means of addressing it.

A major problem in the introduction of new technology is the difficulty of assigning priority in the library budget for the costs. In some cases, the capital investment can be promptly justified in personnel cost savings. In general this is not the case. In a certain sense, these costs are opportunity costs which provide for significant improvements in operation, including service to the scholarly community. If it is clear that the new technology leads to the ultimate planned linkage, there is little doubt that the scholarly community can be more supportive of the sacrifice needed to achieve this.

The challenges are there, and so are the opportunities to meet them and provide a much better information resource for society as a result. We cannot achieve this goal by dealing with the challenges as solvable within our individual libraries. We need to embrace with enthusiasm the notion of cooperation and collaboration as the guide for the future.

University leadership and foundations are willing to assist in this task, but the library community itself must generate the momentum and sustain it. Library directors must realize the needs, accept the conditions which can lead to satisfying them, and provide from among themselves the individual and collective leadership which is required.

NOTES

1. ARL Statistics 1981–82, compiled by Carol A. Mandel (Washington, D.C.: Association of Research Libraries, 1982); ARL Statistics 1982–83, compiled by Carol A. Mandel and Alexander Lichtenstein (Washington, D.C.: Association of Research Libraries, 1983).

2. Scholarly Communication: The Report of the National Enquiry (Baltimore, Md.: Johns Hopkins University Press, 1979).

3. D. Kent Halstead, Inflation Measures for Schools and Colleges (Washington, D.C.: U. S. Government Printing Office, 1983).

4. Nicola Daval (private communication, February 1984).

5. Council on Library Resources, Inc., A National Periodicals Center: Technical Development Plan (Washington, D.C.: Council on Library Resources, 1978).

5

The Relation between Costs and Services at Academic Libraries

Paul B. Kantor

ACADEMIC LIBRARIES: A FUNCTIONAL DESCRIPTION

Academic libraries play a vital role in preparing the leaders of tomorrow. Technologies for storing and retrieving information are changing rapidly, and libraries undergo important changes while maintaining the same basic function. Thus it is important to develop and document a functional view of the academic library.

The functional view (or systems approach) to an operating system describes that system in terms of its goals, environment, inputs, and outputs.[1] For a library, the fundamental goal is to provide access to information. Subsidiary operating goals flow from that major goal. The environment is the college or university. The principal input is budget, while other dynamic inputs (such as materials, staff, and heat) are secondary. It is sometimes helpful to view the physical plant and book stock as a kind of static input.

The outputs of the library are services rendered to the population; library objectives and economic analyses should be expressed in terms of these services. The principal public services are: item lending, in-house use, and staff supported access to information. These output services are supported by a variety of technical processes. Technical processes play an intermediate role: the outputs of technical services are not outputs of the system as a whole.

THE CONCEPT OF A COST FUNCTION

The concept of a cost function originates in the theory of production industries.[2] The key idea is that competing firms will be driven to find the least expensive mix of resources from which they can manufacture a given set of products or provide services. The cost of that mixture of resources is called the cost function of the products or services produced.

The academic library is a nonprofit center operating within a nonprofit institution. There is no dollar market for the primary services. The consumers of library services do not directly buy them. Thus a library cannot modify demand by adjusting prices. In addition, gross revenue is derived not from sales but from a negotiated budget, fixed one or two years in advance. Correspondingly the manager's operating goal is not profit maximization. The agreed upon goal is "maximum service within the available budget." A reasonable guess is that each library director also seeks to increase his budget as much as possible.

The two stages in the economics of academic libraries are distressingly unrelated. First, a budget is set. Second, the library does the best it can to cope with expressed demand while operating within this budget. If the operation of academic libraries is governed by an "invisible hand," it will have evolved in such a way that the budget allocation is the same as the cost function would be for a competitive producer. If such a cost function can be determined, it has three important uses. First, it can guide in the expansion of services so that services do not exceed the capability of the existing budget. Second, it can guide the expansion of budget in connection with projected or observed increases in demand for services. Third, it can be used to motivate library units.

Hence, a study has been carried out to explore the relationship between library expenditures and the services rendered.[3] Three principal services are included in the model: circulation services (C), in-house use of materials (S), and reference services (R). From a mathematical point of view the study is a search for a relationship between the direct budget (BDIR) and the services S, C, R which can be expressed as an equation:

$$BDIR = C(S, C, R) + \text{random variations}$$

Data were gathered at 119 libraries drawn in a two-step random process from the 1979 HEGIS tapes.[4] Mathematical models of a nonlinear form were explored. The best regression fits are obtained with models which mix linear and non-linear effects. The general form of the best equation is

$$C(S, C, R) = (X1^*S + X3^*C + X5^*R + X8)^{X7}$$

The exponent $X7$ is related to economies of scale or increase in returns to scale. If it is greater than one, the cost per unit of service increases with library size. Our best models all indicate that it is slightly greater than one. This would indicate that larger (for example, centralized) libraries have higher unit costs than small libraries. Given the wide variation in actual library costs, we feel that the question must be resolved by a more detailed look at the costs of library services.

The search for a best formula was carried out assuming that the random fluctuations have a multiplicative effect. In practical terms, this determines a formula that gives about the same percentage accuracy for large libraries as it does for small libraries. The coefficients in the three best formulas that we have found are summarized in Table 5.1, which shows three parameter sets giving a good fit to the expense data. Each formula was matched to data from 119 libraries. The wide variation in parameters is due to the multicollinearity of library service data. It is easy to see that there is wide variation in the parameters $X1 - X8$. This is due to the great similarity in mix of services provided by individual libraries (called "multicollinearity"). To study the relationship of individual libraries to the cost formula we interpret the expression inside parenthesis as a load.

Table 5.1

Summary of Coefficients for Three Formulas Discussed Above

	X1	**X3**	**X5**	**X7**	**X8**	**R^2**
I. All para- meters free	2.74 (± 1.19)	0.868 (± 0.35)	1.92 (± 1.15)	1.06 ($\pm .06$)	8.71 (± 4.81)	82%
II. X3, X5 set by factor analysis	2.78	0.83*	3.24*	1.04	9.13	81.8%
III. X3, X5 set by unit cost data	3.60	0.48*	1.54*	1.06	6.76	81.7%

*Value fixed prior to the regression.

$$\text{LOAD} = S + X3^*C + X5^*R$$

The cost formula can then be expressed as

$$\text{BDIR} = X1^*(\text{LOAD} + X8)^{X7}$$

Another way of looking at this is to say that the operating budget, BDIR, defines capacity to serve which, if the model is perfect, is equal to the load. Since the model is not perfect, this capacity, when calculated from the direct budget, will differ from the actual load. The difference between the calculated capacity and the observed load may be expressed as either an apparent reserve capacity or an overload. The range of these variables is shown in a histogram in Figure 5.1.

$$\text{RESERVE} = 100 \times (\text{CAPACITY} - \text{LOAD})/\text{CAPACITY}$$

$$\text{OVERLOAD} = 100 \times (\text{LOAD} - \text{CAPACITY})/\text{CAPACITY}$$

$$\text{CAPACITY} = (\text{BDIR}/X1)^{1/X7} - X8$$

The range is amazingly large. We have explored a number of possible explanations of this range. We have established that the variation is not simply due to the underdetermination of the formula: overloads and reserves are basically unchanged

Figure 5.1.
Histogram of the Overload and Reserve Capacities

420	Wing	
382 302	Wing	
288 270 242 222 204	Wing	Overload (%)
186 161 150 146 113 101	Wing	
89 84 83 83		
79 79 78 78 73 63		
59 58 55 53 47 46 45 41		
39 37 36 34 33 30 28 25 23 23 21 21 21 20		
19 18 17 15 15 13 13 12 11 11 8 7 6 5 5 5 4 4 4 2		
0 – 0		
2 4 5 5 6 6 7 9 10 11 13 13 14 14 16 16 16 16 19 19		
20 23 24 24 25 26 28 28 29 29 30 32 33 33 33 34 34 35 36 36 37 37 38 39		
40 40 41 43 45 47 48 49 50 50 51 52 55 56 57 59 59		
64 66 74 76 78	Wing	Reserve (%)

Note: With this nonlinear model, the mode (most common value) is not at 0, but between 20 and 40 percent reserve capacity. On the other hand 14 libraries have overloads of 100 percent or more. This histogram contains 11 libraries not in our random sample. They were not used in determining the formula.

as the formula is varied. Nor is it due to variation in library size (tested by regression of the reserve capacity on the size), or to special problems in data collection. This enormous variation is not due to subsidiary variables such as type of holdings, degree of net working, public versus private ownership, or degree of computerization. Although these last two variables have a statistically significant effect on the value of $X8$, it is small compared to the range of reserve capacities or overloads. The conclusion is that academic libraries are not operating with direct budgets interpretable as the economic cost function. Something else is determining the budget.

The study found that regression of the direct budget on library holdings (simply expressed as number of monograph volumes plus volumes of bound periodicals), gives a better coefficient of determination, (R-squared = 89%) than any of the output based models. The relationship is very nearly a linear one. Equilibrium of costs and services delivered is not yet achieved, while library budgets are strongly correlated with collection size. This correlation does not in itself explain all deviations from the average formula. Private libraries have a lower average cost curve than public libraries, and computerization of the acquisition/ordering process appears to significantly lower the cost curve.

Overall, academic libraries are quite precariously situated to cope with either a major shift to nonprint media or another fundamental change in the materials to which the libraries provide access. The linkage between holdings and budget has provided a comfortable mode of operations for many years. Coupled with the general similarity in service mix at various libraries, it has permitted libraries to muddle through. As libraries undertake the provision of other types of information service, they will not find it possible to provide needed services with a formula tied to the book stock. The economic viewpoint of libraries must switch from a curatorial, warehousing focus to a focus on the provision of services. The most important tool for obtaining a rational understanding of the relations between costs and services is the determination of unit costs.

UNIT COST DETERMINATIONS: PRESENT RESULTS

Concurrent with the CFAL project,[3] techniques have been developed permitting uniform unit cost analysis for varying libraries.[5] These techniques take into account the fact that nearly all the direct budget contributes to more than one service (book stock and technical services) are a kind of overhead, and that details of cost allocation depend on the actual levels of service rendered. The latter dependence is expressed by a book use equivalency (BUE) factor. The BUE factor represents the number of distinct books which are used in providing a unit of output. It is one for circulation. Based upon interviews with reference librarians (primarily anecdotal evidence) we have taken the average number of items per reference query to be two. Based upon somewhat more systematic, but limited studies of the relationship between reshelving counts and hours of in-house use, we have taken three books per hour as the BUE for in-house use. Owing to the specific mathematics of the unit cost calculation the final results are fairly robust against small variations in the BUE. Note the "use until satisfaction" principle in allocating equal weight to a 20 minute in-house use of a book and the borrowing of a book for weeks or months.

1. All administrative costs are allocated to nonadministrative salaries.

2. Technical services salaries and space (processing, stacks) are added to the direct cost of materials.

3. The resulting sum is allocated to the principal services using the BUE factors.

4. Public service salaries and space costs are added to this allocation.

5. All other direct costs are allocated to these sums.

6. Institutional overhead is allocated to salaries or total costs as appropriate.

7. The total cost of each service is divided by the volume of service delivered.

We have applied this procedure to 30 participating libraries which were willing to take the effort. The results are summarized in Table 5.2. The calculated unit costs show great

Table 5.2
The Unit Cost Summary

		Circulation (number of loans)	Reference (number of queries)	In-house (number of hours of reading)
Average	A	3.72	11.93	7.70
Median	M	3.35	14.00	8.00
Upper 6th	U	6.60	23.00	20.00
Lower 6th	L	1.50	6.00	3.00
(U + L)/2	K	4.05	14.50	11.50

variation, confirming our doubts about the existence of any real equilibrium. It is, however, encouraging to find that the ratio of the mean unit costs, when inserted into the average cost formula, gives a fit essentially as good as the unconstrained fit (see Table 5.1).

Unit cost analysis can determine a valid unit cost formula while the converse is not true, and that unit costs show the wide variation to be expected if the costs of library operation are not yet being determined by the services rendered.

UNIT COSTS: PROSPECTS AND RECOMMENDATIONS

The detailed study of unit costs could shed further light on the problem of economies of scale if the data were not so widely scattered.

Future studies of the economics of academic libraries should build upon the uniform analysis of unit costs. Detailed comparison of the contributing factors to unit costs, within and between institutions, will provide a rational basis for modification of service level, budgets, or both. Detailed analysis of unit cost is needed to extract the management information necessary to a cost function.

Through a sampling study of the economics of academic libraries, a specific determination of the unit costs at a subsample of 30 libraries, as shown in Table 5.2 has been reported. A "statistically impressive" fit given by the nonlinear capacity model with slight diseconomies of scale and no economies of scope is shown! The coefficients of the model are not uniquely determined by the available data, owing to the degree of similarity in the mix of services provided by academic libraries.

The most important results of the study for the economic future of academic libraries are not in these detailed econometric results. The most important conclusion is that the management of academic libraries appears to suffer the worst ill effects of the absence of any kind of a competitive market. Although libraries may compete with each other in a sporting fashion (as indicated by rank in lists of libraries, according to budget, or holdings, or institutional size), the consumers of academic library services have no recourse if one library is more costly than another. In fact, consumers do now know the cost because they do not pay. This may account for the enormous variation of academic libraries around the average cost formula. With improvements in management techniques, and an evolution in the nature of the materials to which academic libraries provide access, the present lack of relation between budgets and services is fraught with dangers. The academic library community should rigorously explore the study of its own costs of operation in relation to services, and work toward a cost function which will provide a far more accurate description of library operations and will serve as a basis for the rational allocation of library funds.

NOTES

This paper is a condensed form of a preliminary report that was prepared for the conference on "Contemporary Issues in Academic and Research Libraries." It was supported in part by the National Science Foundation under Grant IST–8110510. All of these reports are based on the study "Cost Function for Academic Libraries." Any opinions, findings, conclusions or recommendations expressed in this report are those of the author, and do not necessarily reflect the views of the National Science Foundation.

It is a pleasure to acknowledge the support of the NSF Program Officers, Helene Ebenfield and Dr. Charles Brownstein. At Tantalus vital contributions were made by: Judith Wood who coordinated all contact with the participating libraries until July 1983, and did much of the data reduction; Marla Bush who did the unit cost analyses, much of the data reduction, and the typing of reports; Prasert Shusang who did the nonlinear regression analyses, and econometric calculations; Jung Jin Lee who did the national extrapolations, and studies of parameter variance; Michael Hurley who did the nonlinear dynamical analysis; also Linda Karaffa and Kenneth Cruthers for programming. On the Advisory Committee thanks to: Millicent Abell, Richard Talbot, Jacob Cohen, and Robert Hayes. For advice on optimization techniques thanks to: Professor Leon Lasdon of the University of Texas-Austin, and Professor Gerald Saidel of Case Western Reserve University. Thanks to the staff and directors of all the libraries, listed in note 3, and also to those who wish to remain anonymous.

1. Churchman, C. West, *The Systems Approach* (New York: Delacorte Press, 1968).

2. See any textbook on microeconomics. The classic reference for contemporary mathematical economics is: Paul A. Samuelson, *Foundations of Economic Analysis*, enlarged ed. (Cambridge: Harvard University Press, 1983).

3. This is a condensed version of the chapter "Overview" in the report "An Average Expense Formula for Academic Libraries: The Final Report of the CFAL Project" by Paul B. Kantor with Judith Wood, Marla Bush, Prasert Shusang, and Jung Jin Lee. The full report is available from Tantalus Inc., Suite 218, 2140 Lee Road, Cleveland, Ohio 44118.

4. We worked directly from the tapes. The survey has been published in summary form: Beazley, Richard M., *Library Statistics of Colleges and Universities, 1979: Institutional Data* (National Center for Educational Statistics). Available as NTIS publication number PB82–169087.

5. A concurrent study of Health Science Libraries has produced comparable data for 95 health sciences libraries, of which 15 are located at academic institutions. Details will appear in: Kantor, Paul B, "Cost and Usage of Medical Libraries I: Economic Aspects" submitted to the *Bulletin of the Medical Library Association*.

6

Twenty Years after Clapp-Jordan: A Review of Academic Library Funding Formulas

Daniel W. Lester

Academic library administrators have used a variety of formulas to assess the adequacy of their libraries since the 1920s or earlier. The Carnegie Commission developed a formula in 1928 and the American Library Association followed with its own formula in 1930. These formulas inspired some interest, but perhaps owing to the overwhelming financial problems of the depression and war that followed, there was little serious formula development for several decades to come. The first formulas to become of major importance to academic libraries were the ones included in the Association of College and Research Libraries (ACRL) standards of 1959.[1] These standards first suggested two major formula funding concepts that are still widely used today: a percentage of the college's educational and general budget that should be allocated to the library and a minimal collection size for the library that was determined by an opening collection plus a component determined by enrollment.

The Clapp-Jordan formula was first published in 1964[2] and more widely disseminated in 1965.[3] This formula expanded on the concepts presented in the 1959 ACRL standards for collection size by adding components for the number and level of degree programs offered by the college or university. This new component has been used by a wide variety of formulas since that time and has inspired a great deal of discussion among librarians and administrators. The Clapp-Jordan formula was adopted by many librarians and state higher education commissions to assist them in assessing the adequacy of the libraries under their charge, determining needs, and formulating budget requests. A number of variations and modifications in the Clapp-Jordan formula were developed by individuals and committees during the late 1960s and early 1970s, and widely discussed at library conferences and meetings. At least one conference devoted to formula funding was held in 1974 in Minnesota. After a number of committee meetings and drafts, the Association of College and Research Libraries adopted new standards for college libraries in 1975.[4] The collection size standard published by ACRL, which is an updating of the Clapp-Jordan formula, is essentially the same as that developed by the state of Washington. Although librarians have seemed to be generally satisfied with these standards, and many have used them in budget requests, there is still no widespread acceptance of them by higher education commissions, and the ACRL has another committee now working to develop new standards for college libraries.

METHODOLOGY

In the fall of 1973 Dale Carrison and the author surveyed the higher education commissions of the 50 states in order to collect background information to assist in the development of a draft formula for funding state college libraries in Minnesota.[5] At that time 37 commissions responded, indicating that 20 used formulas of some type for library funding and 17 used no library formulas. The author presented a summary of this survey at the American Library Association Conference in 1974 and distributed a bibliography of the formulas that had been identified at that time.[6]

In the spring of 1979 the author was requested by the New Mexico Board of Educational Finance (the higher education commission for the state) to conduct a similar survey to help the board in determining whether New Mexico should develop its own library funding formula. After an intensive campaign of letters and telephone calls, responses were obtained from all fifty states. At that time, 19 states indicated that they were using some type of library formula and 31 were using no library formulas. This information was presented to the administration of the University of New Mexico Library and the New Mexico Board of Educational Finance, but no library formula was subsequently adopted in New Mexico.[7]

During the fall of 1980 Mary P. McKeown surveyed the higher education commissions of the states by letter and telephone to determine for the Maryland State Board for Higher Education the usage of formulas and guidelines of all types for higher education funding in other states. Her report for the board indicated that 26 states had used formulas or guidelines for library funding during the 1977–1980 period.[8] Her results were subsequently published in a more accessible form as an article in *Journal of Education Finance*.[9]

In the fall of 1983 the author again surveyed the fifty state higher education commissions by letter, ultimately receiving 30 responses. Of those states responding, only 9 said they were using formulas for library funding, while 21 stated that they used no library formulas, although some of these 21 used formulas in other areas of higher education. The disappointing response rate may have been due to the lack of an official sanction from a state higher education commission for the request, a lower level of follow-up than in other surveys, or a lack of interest in formula funding for libraries by the higher education commissions.

The results of all of these surveys were compiled and compared to provide an overview of the usage of library formulas by higher education commissions for the last ten years. The section following provides information about the compilation and tabulation.

RESULTS

All of the information obtained from the various states in these four surveys is summarized in Table 6.1. The columns labeled 1983, 1979, and 1973 indicate responses to the author's surveys in the respective years. The column labeled

Table 6.1
Library Funding Formula Usage in the 50 States, 1973–83

State	1983	1977–80	1979	1973
Alabama	No response	Rate per credit hour by level	Rate per credit hour by level	Rate per credit hour
Alaska	No response	Use a guideline	None	No response
Arizona	No response	No response	None	None
Arkansas	No response	Rate per FTE added to base by institution type	Rate per credit hour by level over base	Rate per credit hour
California	No response	No response	None	Generates dollars only
Colorado	None	None	None	Generates staff plus 5% growth rate
Connecticut	No response	No response	None	None
Delaware	No response	No response	None	None
Florida	No response	Rate per FTE	Modified Washington formula	Modified Washington formula
Georgia	No response	9% of primary programs	9% of instruction and general	9% of instruction and general
Hawaii	No response	No response	None	No response
Idaho	No response	No response	None	No response
Illinois	None	No response	None	None
Indiana	None	No response	None	No response
Iowa	None	No response	None	None
Kansas	None	Rate per FTE by level	Rate per FTE by level	Rate per FTE by level

Table 6.1 *(continued)*

State	1983	1977–80	1979	1973
Kentucky	Rate per credit hour, with a minimum	Rate per credit hour by level, with addition for small colleges	Rate per credit hour by level, with addition for small colleges	None
Louisiana	5% of educational and general	5% of instructional costs	5% of educational and general	No response
Maine	No response	No response	None	None
Maryland	Rate per credit hour by level and size, with a minimum	Rate per credit hour by level	None	Generates staff only
Massachusetts	No response	No response	None	No response
Michigan	No response	No response	None	No response
Minnesota	None	None	None	None
Mississippi	None	Included in instructional guideline	None	No response
Missouri	6% of educational and general	Included in administrative guideline	Rate per FTE for universities, fixed amount for small colleges	No response
Montana	None	No response	None	None
Nebraska	None	No response	None	None
Nevada	No response	None	None	Washington formula
New Hampshire	None	No response	None	No response
New Jersey	None	Included in instructional guideline	None	No response

Table 6.1 *(continued)*

State	1983	1977–80	1979	1973
New Mexico	None	None	None	None
New York	Use a guideline	Use a guideline	None	None
North Carolina	None	No response	None	None
North Dakota	No response	Rate per FTE by institution type	None	Rate per FTE
Ohio	None	Included in instructional guideline	Included as part of academic support	Generates dollars only
Oklahoma	No response	Included in instructional support	7% of budget	7% of budget
Oregon	No response	Washington formula	Washington formula	No response
Pennsylvania	None	Included in instructional guideline	None	None
Rhode Island	None	No response	None	No response
South Carolina	10% of total instructional costs	10% of total instructional costs	10% of total instructional costs	Generates dollars only
South Dakota	None	Rate per FTE for books, plus salaries	9.5% instructional programs	Generates dollars only
Tennessee	Rate per credit hour by level and subject	Rate per credit hour by level	Rate per credit hour by level	Rate per credit hour by level
Texas	Rate per credit hour by level	Rate per credit hour by level	Rate per credit hour by level	Rate per credit hour by level
Utah	None	No response	None	Generates staff only

Table 6.1 (continued)

State	1983	1977–80	1979	1973
Vermont	None	No response	None	None
Virginia	No response	Staff per FTE by level and type, Washington formula for collections	Staff per FTE by level and type, Washington formula for collections	Staff formula and 5% growth rate for collections
Washington	Rate per student	1978 formula, regression based	1978 formula, regression based	1970 formula, Clapp-Jordan based
West Virginia	None	Percent of base by type of institution	None	Generates staff only
Wisconsin	None	Percentage of instructional costs, added to a base	Washington as a guideline	5% of instructional costs
Wyoming	No response	No response	None	None

1977–1980 contains information obtained from McKeown's survey which asked whether the respondents had used formulas during that four-year period. Table 6.1 is a very brief summary.

Since 1973 twenty states have not used formulas for library budgeting. These states, Arizona, Connecticut, Delaware, Hawaii, Idaho, Illinois, Indiana, Iowa, Maine, Massachusetts, Michigan, Minnesota, Montana, Nebraska, New Hampshire, New Mexico, North Carolina, Rhode Island, Vermont, and Wyoming, include all of the New England states and a scattering of states from the midwest and west. Only one southern state, North Carolina, did not use some sort of library formula in the past decade.

Another nine states, almost all located in the south, have used a rate per credit hour or rate per FTE (full-time equivalent student) formula during the 1973–1983 decade. Six of them, Alabama, Arkansas, Florida, North Dakota, Tennessee, and Texas, used a formula of this type throughout the period. Three others, Kansas, Kentucky, and Maryland, began the use of such a formula since 1973, although Kansas discontinued the use of the formula in 1983. Rate per credit hour and rate per FTE formulas are treated as the same type of formula owing to the linear relationship between credit hours and full-time equivalent students in a given state. Comparing funding between states, however, is more difficult owing to the differences in how states compute full-time equivalency. Some states use quarter hours while others use semester hours. The number of hours required to produce one FTE varies by state and, in many states, by level of the student. Owing to this lack of comparability, the rates used by the states are not presented in Table 6.1.

Six states, also predominantly from the south, used a percentage formula for academic library funding during the 1973–1983 decade. All six, Georgia, Louisiana, Oklahoma, South Carolina, West Virginia, and Wisconsin, used a percentage of educational and general, instructional and general, or a similar designation. Most of these states did not specify exactly what is included in such a category in their budget, however, so making comparisons is once again difficult. For example, it is unlikely that Georgia funds libraries at a rate almost double that of Louisiana, despite the indication that Georgia funds libraries at 9 percent of instruction and general and Louisiana funds them at 5 percent of educational and general. Even with access to complete budget documents it is difficult to determine the exact comparison of budgets from one state to another. Since 1979 the states of Wisconsin and West Virginia have dropped the use of a formula of this type and use no formula at present.

One state, Missouri, changed from a rate per FTE formula for its larger colleges in 1973, to an administrative guideline in the later 1970s, to a percentage of base in 1983. The current Missouri 6 percent of educational and general is supplemented by the recommendation of appropriations which would place Missouri at the median among universities of similar size and academic mission. Informal communications have indicated that many academic libraries use comparisons of this type to support budget requests to campus administrators, even if the type of comparison is not officially recognized by a higher education commission. The usual problem with comparisons of this type is reaching agreement regarding which institutions comprise the peer group for one's own. Some schools have decided that the peer group is composed of the members of the intercollegiate athletic conference group to which they belong, a comparison that seems offensive to many librarians at first. Since most athletic conferences are composed of institutions of similar size and type of governance, this method of determining a peer group may be better than it appears at first glance.

Several states have developed their own formulas in recent years. California and Colorado used their own formulas in the early 1970s, but had dropped them by 1977. The California formula served as a key component in the development of the Washington formula, the most successful and widely used formula. The Washington formula for collection size is an updated version of the Clapp-Jordan formula, and it has been adopted as published or modified by several states. Florida used it to determine collection adequacy for several years, and Oregon still uses it in this manner. Nevada used the Washington formula until 1975, when it was dropped because the legislature ignored the formula. Many states have compared their collections to the Washington formula or to its successor, the 1975 ACRL formula. None of the states surveyed, however, indicated that it used the ACRL formula in budget planning. Other states that have used their own formulas at some time since 1973 include Virginia, South Dakota, and Utah. Of these three, only Virginia is still using any formula at this time.

The remaining states, Alaska, Mississippi, New Jersey, New York, Pennsylvania, and Ohio, have used "guidelines" for library funding at various times in the last ten years. Mississippi and Ohio have dropped guidelines recently while the others continue their use. McKeown asked higher education commissions about the use of guidelines as well as the use of formulas, which is at least one reason for the differences between her responses for the 1977–1980 period and the responses the author received to the 1979 survey. Some states consider guidelines and formulas to be the same thing, while others consider that they are different. What one state considers a guideline might be a formula to another state, and vice versa. Most commissions appear to consider formulas to be more precise and prescriptive than guidelines. Until the terminology is clarified and standardized there will continue to be confusion in this area.

ANALYSIS

The number of states using some type of library funding formula for institutions of higher education reached at least 20 in 1973 and has stayed at approximately the same level since that time. Thirteen states kept the same method of funding throughout the 1973–1983 decade, while 17 others added, dropped, or changed their funding method during the period. Twenty states avoided any use of formula funding throughout the decade.

Despite the appearance of a number of proposed funding, collection size, and collection growth formulas in the last ten years, including those by Voight,[10] Spyers-Duran,[11] and Stubbs,[12] none of them has been widely adopted, if adopted at all. No single funding, collection, or staffing formula has been adopted by more than three or four states at any one time. Even the state of Washington, which has used its own formulas since 1970, changed its formulas over the years and may change them again in the near future. Washington stated that it is currently reviewing its latest formula with the goal of greater simplification of the formula. The reasons for dropping or avoiding formulas in some of the states that do not use them suggest some of the problems with formula usage. Connecticut rejected the use of the Clapp-Jordan formula several years ago because it suggested that needs were so great that the formula was unacceptable. Illinois formally used the Clapp-Jordan formula as a reference point, but more recently dropped that usage because it was decided that formulas did not work. Montana expressed an interest in formulas, but

ceased use over 10 years ago because formulas were too sophisticated for legislative purposes. Nevada had a similar experience, dropping the Washington formula in 1975 because
the legislature ignored the formula. Nebraska never adopted
formulas because the legislative political process is considered
to be the appropriate method of funding libraries and other
institutions.

Although the use of library funding formulas has remained
fairly constant, there seems to be an impending decline in their
use, based on comments received from several state higher
education commissions. Formulas which are reasonable models
of academic libraries or which require sophisticated statistical
techniques appear to be too complex to use effectively in the
legislative and political arenas. In many cases, they appear to
be too complex for campus administrators and some librarians. Although continued statistical analysis may lead to improved models of academic libraries, it remains for others to
determine how to successfully adapt these models to the political arena if funding formulas are to survive.

NOTES

1. "ALA Standards for College Libraries," *College and Research
Libraries* 20 (July 1959): 274–80.

2. Verner W. Clapp and Robert T. Jordan, *The Libraries of the
State-assisted Institutions of Higher Education in Ohio, Their Maintenance and Development: Guidelines for Policy* (Washington: Council on Library Resources, 1964).

3. Verner W. Clapp and Robert T. Jordan, "Quantitative Criteria
for Adequacy of Academic Library Collections," *College and Research
Libraries* 26: (Sept. 1965): 371–80.

4. "Standards for College Libraries," *College and Research Libraries News* 9: (Oct. 1975): 278–301.

5. Minnesota State College System Media Directors, "A Media
Resources and Services Budgetary Analysis and Allocation System
for Minnesota Higher Education Institutions, Draft III" (Mankato:
Mankato State College Media System, 1965, photocopied).

6. Daniel W. Lester, "Bibliography of Library Budgeting, Staffing, and Collection Evaluation Formulas" (Lincoln: University of Nebraska Libraries, 1974, photocopied).

7. Daniel W. Lester, "Summary of Library Formulas" (Albuquerque: University of New Mexico Libraries, 1980, photocopied).

8. Maryland State Board for Higher Education, *Use of Budget Guidelines Among the States* (Annapolis: Maryland State Board for Higher Education, 1981).

9. Mary P. McKeown, "The Use of Formulas for State Funding of Higher Education," *Journal of Education Finance* 7: (Winter 1982): 277–300.

10. Melvin J. Voigt, "Acquisition Rates in University Libraries," *College and Research Libraries* 36: (July 1975): 263–71.

11. Peter Spyers-Duran, "Prediction of Resource Needs: a Model Budget Formula for Upper Division University Libraries" (Ed.D. diss., Nova University, 1975); Peter Spyers-Duran, "Proposed Model Budget Analysis System and Quantitative Standards for the Libraries of the Nebraska State Colleges" (Boca Raton: the Author, 1973, photocopied, ED 077 529).

12. Kendon Stubbs, "University Libraries: Standards and Statistics," *College and Research Libraries* 42 (Nov. 1981): 577–38.

7

Financial Planning: New Needs, New Sources, New Styles

Murray S. Martin

Traditionally, academic libraries have been regarded as an overhead cost by their parent institutions. Although this attitude has lent them a kind of spurious independence, that independence has been costly. Costly, that is, not in the sense of loss of income, but in the divorce that results from general planning and budgetary processes. Instead of developing measures that link the library to the general goals of the institution, libraries have developed a series of quantitative measures, usually based on collection-size or number of transactions. Any cross-checking that related these measures to other academic activities, such as research and teaching, has at best been nebulous. In such circumstances, it is easy to approach library financing in an arbitrary way, since cuts and changes are not seen in relation to other institutional goals, hence the stories that circulate about devastating cuts in the acquisitions budget and the equally difficult problems caused by sudden year-end windfalls.

The second major planning problem results from being budget- rather than program- or output-driven. The goal of retaining or increasing a budget is substantially different from the goal of maintaining or changing programs. Since most budgets remain essentially line item despite attempts to introduce zero-base or program budgeting, justifications are sought in terms of specific items rather than their products. If, in addition, strict control is exercised in terms of individual budget lines, any attempt to introduce major changes or shifts of emphasis may be doomed from the beginning.

To some extent, both these factors have had less effect than might have been expected. While the library was regarded as a warehouse, its problems were seen, by libraries and administrators, principally in terms of how much they could buy and house, and incremental budgeting generally managed to cope with this kind of development. Gradually, however, libraries and user expectations have changed until the old pattern of funding has become inadequate. These changes relate principally to the extension of services and technologies, both of which require a very different approach. Second, at the same time as libraries began to extend automation, their parent institutions, for a wide variety of causes, have become less able to finance expansion. Uncertain student enrollments, rapid changes in academic needs, loss of federal income, and increased pressure on state budgets have combined to create an atmosphere in which traditional expenditures are increasingly questioned. Accountability, cost benefits, and more directed planning result. To meet these changes libraries have had to reexamine their financial base and their modes of financial planning. Finally, in times when institutions are forcing the pace, requiring faculty members to seek grants and outside funding to replace other lost revenue, when entire departments may be terminated and the resources redirected, libraries cannot expect to be left unscathed.

In the face of all these institutional changes, what must librarians do? The first and most urgent need is a total reconsideration of library goals. Such a reconsideration cannot be carried out autonomously. Integration into university planning processes is essential. This change is required because of the need to show how library services (products) are linked to academic products. This need, in turn, requires that libraries develop new measures which reflect use and need, rather than quantitative library-oriented measures. There is, after all, a purpose behind the building of collections and the provision of user-services and that purpose requires highlighting if adequate funding is to be assured. One of the snags in such a process is that the benefits derived from library services are diffuse, difficult to aggregate, and therefore difficult to relate directly to individual academic programs. Even a branch library, which might seem a clear case of program-related library activity, is supported by other library expenditures and serves other academic programs than those of the departments it relates to most directly. The underlying problem is that the taxonomic arrangements of library and university, though superficially similar, are, in fact, fundamentally different and any attempt to match them in detail is doomed to failure. Nevertheless, library costs should be assigned to academic areas, grouping together similar departments. This was the unexpressed rationale behind the divisional concept of libraries and it was an admirable attempt at the assignment of library costs. What is now required is that the principle behind it be refined and extended.

In order to do this, libraries need to reexamine the services they provide in terms of inputs and outputs (unpleasant but necessary words) to show more clearly what they contribute to their supporting institutions. The term added value is preferred since that is appropriate to the role of middleman in the information transfer process. The two parts of this term can be combined quite satisfactorily. The principal role of a library is to collect and organize information. The inputs consist of discrete pieces of data, acquired, leased, or accessed, the work required to organize these, and provision for dissemination services. The outputs consist of a wide variety of access services—circulation, reference, data-base searches, bibliographies, and so on. The added value derives from the effort spent in organizing otherwise unorganized information. It is this added value that justifies the existence of the library and hence its cost. It is, therefore, necessary to structure financial planning (and all the associated presentations) to demonstrate this added value. Library budgets have traditionally been divided into categories—personnel, library acquisitions, and other expenditures—which disguise this product. For a variety of control reasons, line budgets will continue to be needed for operational purposes. For planning and budget development, however, they are totally inadequate, nor, for other reasons, are the usual program budgets much better since they tend to be couched in organizational rather than product terms. Instead, it is necessary to adopt a kind of matrix presentation which incorporates all three goals. Naturally, such an objective cannot be achieved without some hard work, but the results should be significant in terms of increased understanding. Without such understanding, libraries will continue to be regarded as financial bottomless pits.

INTEGRATION OF OBJECTIVES

First, it is necessary to integrate library and institutional objectives. Most academic institutions have difficulty in articulating their objectives clearly, which is understandable but dangerous since uncertainty in what the institution wishes to achieve makes it almost impossible for support services even to begin shaping their own objectives. Nevertheless, most institutions define their priorities, even by not making decisions, simply by the investment they make in faculty, assisted, of course, by students who show quite clearly their own objectives by the courses they persistently over- or under-enroll. It is possible, by examining the resulting institutional profile, to determine what the institution's goals appear to be. The word appear is used because in many instances past tenure decisions distort present intentions. Refinement is possible by taking into account other expenditures. Where, for example, is the institution making important investments in buildings, computers, and support services? Fuzzy as the resulting picture frequently is, it is usually possible to distinguish clearly between major and minor commitments, and it is with these that libraries must be most concerned. One lesson that has to be driven home again and again is the high cost of supporting programs in science and technology. An analysis of library expenditures in terms of the university's own taxonomy is usually a very instructive exercise.

Most libraries are finding it increasingly difficult to provide on the spot the material resources their clients have become accustomed to, yet they have not begun seriously to grapple with the budgetary implications of the alternatives. One reason is that librarians are still accustomed to thinking of the acquisitions budget as a program, separate from all the other kinds of expenditures libraries might expect to make each year. In fact, it has never had such an independent existence, even though budgetary authorities and librarians have acted as if that were so. The decision to buy so many materials has staff and space implications that affect the entire library operation, while a choice between different levels of financial support can have unforeseen effects on academic programs, because of the differential costs and price increases in different areas.

To put this for a moment in a clear, if hypothetical, financial framework let us take a medium-sized academic library. This will be my stalking horse for a number of other proposals. (Refer to Appendix.) In order to spend $1,000,000 on library materials, our library must commit annually $400,000 in salaries; $80,000 in contracted services; at least $20,000 in other office costs; $40,000 on repairs, renovations, equipment, and maintenance; probably $20,000 or more in staff time spent on selection; and a further $20,000 in other office costs and administrative overhead. The total library cost of the acquisitions program is thus $1,580,000 without taking account of such costs as first time shelving of new materials, or the longer-range cost of amortized space to house continually growing collections. Since the total number of volumes added averages 20,000 per year, of which 12,000 are newly purchased monographs and 8,000 are bound volumes of periodicals, the cost per volume added is even more significant than the total added cost.

If, therefore, the institution wishes to increase the rate of growth of the collections, the cost of doing so will differ considerably according to the numbers and mixes of materials acquired, but fundamental to it is the recognition that more than materials costs is at issue. Moreover, at maximum shelving capacity each added 20 volumes require 1 square foot of new building space at a minimum furnished cost of $150. To purchase and shelve 20,000 volumes is to use up 1,000 square feet of space for a cost of $150,000. Because the new space used is spread through a number of buildings its annual effect is not

Cost per Volume Added

	Monographs	Serials
Material costs	$25	$70
Binding	negligible	10
Processing costs	35	20
Totals	60	100

so dramatic. Indeed, most libraries are built with many years of expansion room included and it is only toward the end of that span that the problem reemerges. Nevertheless, at a given future time it will become necessary to choose between adding new collection space and displacing readers or services in favor of books (both of which are expensive and difficult options) or discovering some new way to provide dynamic balance between expanding collections and services and static physical space.

All this underlines the fact that decisions concerning the future are never simple and clear-cut, if only for the reason that we can never foresee in detail what has not yet happened. In the case presented there are two evident factors: the university has to recognize that academic library support is not simply a matter of book budgets and the library has to recognize that it must present a new pathway to the future if it is to reconcile budgetary constraints with program needs. One possible direction to follow is to substitute the notion of access for that of possession. In the case of the hypothetical library described, possession turns out to be a progressively more expensive option. Until recently, the alternatives to possession were very limited. Interlibrary loan on a large scale is impractical, not because it cannot be done, but because it is laborious (even with electronic help) and slow. It is also increasingly expensive as use fees are imposed. Use privileges in other libraries can help, but only in situations where the other libraries are close by and committed to cooperation. Moreover, few libraries are in a position to permit large-scale borrowing by outsiders. Electronic publishing, though still in its infancy, offers a new way of access. A prime example is the new program of article access offered by University Microforms International. Another is the down loading program offered by Chemical Abstracts. For argument's sake suppose that the library decided to dedicate as much as 10 percent ($100,000) of its materials budget to alternative access. This implies a reduction in processing costs of up to $50,000 which can be redirected to support of the new program. For such an expenditure it is possible to purchase the requisite hardware, say three or four microcomputers, pay for the costs of maintenance and transmission, add staff to interlibrary loan and reference and provide both on-line reference access free of charge and personal copies of needed articles. Books are not yet so amenable to such treatment, but it is also possible to purchase inexpensive books (say paperbacks) outside the library's collection profile for giving to those who need them, on the basis that the library's role is to provide needed information, rather than to collect against hypothetical future need. A long-term indirect savings is a reduction in the need for new space. Of course, it is a risky step and runs counter to tradition *and* it destroys one of the principal measures of library success—collection growth. Nevertheless, it increases the measure of success in meeting actual need, by guaranteeing access to materials not officially part of the collection. Such a move was not possible without such a guarantee and was never possible when interlibrary loan was the *only* alternative.

NEW BUDGETARY CONCEPTS

This way of operating also introduces a totally new concept to library budgeting: the cost of user access. At present, there is no way of arriving accurately at the cost to the user of using the library; ways to measure this cost must be found if successful cost-benefit analysis of alternatives is to be made. One crude estimate may be made by figuring the cost of faculty time spent in using the library. As a proportion of the total faculty salaries paid this is not an insignificant cost and any way that use of time can be made more efficient and effective is beneficial to the university. In fact, this is one of the principal benefits of automation since the wider distribution of catalog and circulation information it makes possible can reduce considerably the amount of time wasted in looking for resources, particularly as it becomes possible to perform much initial searching from an office terminal. The changes introduced by automation should be examined and presented from this perspective. Seen in this light, the capital expenditure represented by automation offers the chance of major returns in the shape of library effectiveness. This argument applies not only to the usual components of an automated system but to improvement in reference services achieved by terminal access to dictionaries, encyclopedias, and the many data banks available. Many of these activities must continue to be mediated by librarians and the use of printed resources will continue to play an important role. Nevertheless, the addition of electronic information services adds a flexibility to the library as it seeks to personalize the pursuit of information. It is also possible, because of the records generated, to test more accurately the success of alternatives, and in a way not possible when the preponderance of activity was based on manual procedures.

All such projects require capital investment. The purchase or development of an automated system requires greater capital than libraries can generate internally. Libraries must, therefore, seek outside capital. In some cases, this can be found by parent institutions, if they can be persuaded that the investment is beneficial. Mostly, however, the capital must be sought from donors: alumni, foundations, and corporations. Librarians who have not usually had to play a major role as fund-raisers may find this uncomfortable. Among other effects, it forces consideration of long-term financial planning because projects such as automation can seldom be completed within one budget year. It is equally probable that finance must be sought indirectly if, for example, donors can be found for other purposes such as collection development or renovations of facilities. Institutions have to be persuaded that the relief obtained by such fund-raising should be allowed to free other parts of the budget for the support of automation. This element of flexibility is frequently not available because of strictures built into the budgeting process or because legislatures impose line restrictions. Librarians caught in such a bind must work with their administration to achieve greater flexibility. Very few institutions of higher education have well-developed plans for capital expenditure or even for the maintenance and upkeep of existing capital installation. In the case of public institutions, this is usually because the annual budget is an operating one which makes no allowance for depreciation or capital investment. In private institutions, reliance has generally been placed on special fund-raising efforts or bond issues, all of which must be repaid from tuition. Working a way out of this predicament is not easy. When it is not possible to capitalize savings from an annual budget, there is no incentive to save or to invest in the future. One way is to plan deliberately for annual expenditures for capital purposes. Another is to develop various mechanisms for charge-back or income generation which is not subject to the controls usually exercised over annual operating budgets.

Traditional library budgets—lines for personnel, books, serials, and so on—get in the way of financial planning. Program budgets are a little better, but they tend not to be radical enough, because the organizational structure of the library gets in the way.

A prime case, collection development, is usually perceived as an autonomous activity whose object is to increase the book budget. It also requires consideration of the costs of acquisition, cataloging, processing, shelving, and access, and has never been allied to interlibrary loan, or its recent cousin, data-base searching, yet all of these are part of the resource-finding and providing process, and should be so recognized budgetarily.

In another area, is the shape of the public services programs a help or a hindrance in establishing proper relationships between service and cost? How many reference-points are maintained? Too many, or too few? Is there confusion as to the mix of activities? What relationship is there between reference and circulation? How closely are links maintained with branches? Is there turf jealousy? Very few of these questions could be answered from traditional statistics and yet those answers are essential in establishing the cost information needed to generate appropriate budgets.

Unless we take steps to measure more effectively our performance, it will become increasingly more difficult to justify budget requests and to allocate resources for maximum return on investment.

THE COST OF INFORMATION

Librarians have generally been uncomfortable with any tax on information, quite correctly, because the assignment of marginal costs is both difficult and inequitable. When collection or other information services are in place, the added cost of extra use is, comparatively, negligible. The direct assignment of costs can lead to institutional bickering based on erroneous concepts of cost. Nevertheless, information provision is a significant proportion of the cost of all educational and research programs, and should be recognized as such. A library which is perceived solely as an overhead expenditure is extremely vulnerable to budgetary manipulation. If, however, it is seen as an integral part of each program, its cost is much more easily defended. A university which looks at library costs as a part of new or revised academic programs is much more likely to plan realistically. Similarly, it is possible to develop ways of building information service costs into research grants, rather than simply perceiving them as overhead costs.

Although alternatives in information provision, such as interlibrary loan or electronic information services, should be regarded as part of the resource budget and provided as a common good, there are many items which can and should be regarded as private goods and, therefore, chargeable. What these are can be determined by the use of an added value measure. When services or resources are simply substitutional for those traditionally available they should be free—in the sense that they are provided from the common pool. The same is true when they result in costs foregone, as in processing costs. When, however, they represent an additional service, as is true in the provision of extensive data-base searching, they represent private goods which are chargeable.

OUTSIDE SERVICES

An entire area of service that must be reconsidered is service to users outside the primary constituency. Sometimes, as is frequently the case in interlibrary loan, these are balanced by services received. Even here, however, the problem of the net lending library requires a mechanism for reimbursement. States are frequently able to arrange appropriate methods of subvention, while programs such as those of medical libraries are based on standard costs where coupons or similar units of exchange are used to provide reimbursement. Other institutions have had to initiate charges designed to limit external use. All such mechanisms are cumbersome and result in greatly increased record-keeping costs. Several institutions have instituted fee-based services to outsiders, such as industry and business. This may vary from the approach adopted by institutions like Rice and Lehigh universities, where services have been aggressively marketed, to the approach adopted by the Countway Library of Medicine, which instituted personal and corporate charges designed to reduce external use. Other institutions have adopted a fee-based approach in serving allied, quasi-independent research institutes. Most common, however, is the practice of imposing a differential surcharge on outside recipients of such services as data-base searching. Even in public institutions a difference may be made between the use of the library and borrowing privileges, the former usually being free, the latter subject to annual fee. Libraries with special products, such as photographs or genealogical records, may impose fees for reproduction in these areas while continuing to provide other services free-of-charge. Variable as these practices are, they are becoming common enough to establish some pattern. The classical income from fees, fines, and booksales is being supplemented by a wide range of services bearing a charge which includes the reimbursement not only of material costs but of personnel and other overhead recoveries. This trend can be expected to intensify. It is now considered reasonable to attempt to recover costs proportionate to the amount of service given to others. While the amount may be relatively small, the goal of recovering 5 percent or even 10 percent of a library's cost is not a minor one. Mechanisms such as associate library memberships (usually for a substantial fee which includes, for example, a certain number of free searches) are becoming more common, particularly for specialized libraries, such as law, business or medicine, while internal special services may be provided only for a fee.

Regularization of such practices, and the consequent projection of expected income, should become a standard part of financial planning. In the same way, projections of capital need must be built into financial plans. Automation is fine, but terminals do not live forever and require replacement on a regular basis. The rapidly increasing numbers and kinds of equipment required by modern libraries have resulted in substantial shifts between budgetary categories. Whereas in traditional libraries the amount of expenditure for items other than materials and personnel seldom exceeded 10 percent and was frequently lower, it is clear from examination of available statistics, particularly the annual reports of the Association of Research Libraries, that the old rules about proportions no longer apply, and the category of support expenditures can be expected to reach 15 percent or higher. Unless new income can be acquired to balance this increase, then expenditures elsewhere will continue to be reduced. The reduction will not necessarily be absolute. It is more likely to be relative unless the institution itself experiences severe financial dislocations and decreases the library budget. Here the classic situation of the serial budget will repeat itself, since systems, once installed, have to be maintained. This is a major reason for increased emphasis on seeking external income and external grants and gifts. Since grants and gifts, of their nature, are temporary unless they are sufficiently large to establish an endowment, their uncertainty can be expected to increase the emphasis on the seeking of more or less permanent external income sources.

THE MARKETING OF THE LIBRARY

Marketing approaches to the provisions of library services must be managed and packaged to make them attractive to potential users. That, in turn, implies the expenditure of developmental money.

Libraries have seldom undertaken much in the way of public relations. There is a pervasive failure to keep the faculty informed. Apparently most scholars are unaware of and consequently undervalue the library infrastructure needed to supply their information needs, hence their persistent support of increases in the book budget, unaccompanied by any recognition of the need for processing and reference assistance. We have neglected a potential constituency and must hasten to remedy this defect.

Publicity, fund-raising events, and newsletters can be expected to play a larger part in library activities and consequently in their budgets, which, of course, means provision for their cost. Spending money is a new idea for most libraries—and for many institutions as well—but it is necessary. Even the act of financial planning costs money and one may expect to see more library appointments of budget and business officers and planning assistants. While libraries are no more businesses than are their parent institutions, they do generate products and librarians will have to learn to recognize the costs associated with their generation. To some extent the package is the message and our packaging is usually as old-fashioned as most of the books on our shelves. In turn this implies differentiating between real and false products which leads us back to our point of entry. The first step in financial planning is to examine and evaluate programs and goals. Until this is done no true planning can take place.

APPENDIX: THE EVER-HOPEFUL
UNIVERSITY LIBRARIES

Total annual university expenditure for general and educational purposes: $100,000,000

Number of students: 5,000 undergraduate
                        500 graduate
                        2,000 professional (Medical, Dental, Allied Health)

Number of faculty: 500 FTE

Number of U.G. Majors: 55

Number of MA programs: 15

Number of PhD programs 20   (includes two regionally unique programs)

Number of Professional 4   (includes professional degree in Engineering)
    Programs

Total annual expenditure on university libraries $3,000,000

Of which $50,000 derives from endowments
         $25,000 from state support for designated programs

    and $50,000 from various income sources - fines, fees, sales

There are three major library buildings and three small branches.

Existing Library Budget

Grouped expenditures are:

Personnel (including fringe benefits)	$1,600,000	(54%)
Library Materials	$1,000,000	(33%)
Support expenditures	$ 400,000	(13%)
Total	$3,000,000	

Library materials expenditures are apportioned thus:

Serials	$560,000
Books	300,000
Other (AV Micro etc.)	60,000
Binding	80,000
	$1,000,000

Personnel Expenditures are apportioned thus:

University Library Administration		$100,000
General Administration (Libraries A,B, & C)		$100,000

Technical Services:

Library A	$250,000	
Library B	50,000	
Library C	100,000	$400,000

Reference

Library A	300,000	
Library B	50,000	
Library C	100,000	$450,000

Circulation and Reserve

Library A	150,000	
Library B	50,000	
Library C	50,000	$250,000

Special Services (Docs/Spec Collection)

Library A	$200,000	
Library B	-	
Library C	-	$200,000

Support Services (Automation, Collection Development/AV etc)

Library A	$100,000	$100,000

$1,600,000

Support Expenditures are apportioned thus

General Office costs		$60,000

Automation costs (OCLC & Contracted Services)

Library A	$50,000	
Library B	$10,000	
Library C	$20,000	$80,000
Travel & staff development	$20,000	
Equipment	$80,000	
Repairs & Renovations	$80,000	
Telephone & Communications	$30,000	
Maintenance Costs	$40,000	
Memberships	$10,000	$400,000
	TOTAL:	$3,000,000

Restructured Library Budget

Grouped expenditures are:

Personnel	$1,650,000
Library Resources: Materials	$ 900,000
Access Services	$ 50,000
Support expenditures	$ 500,000
TOTAL	$3,100,000
Less new externally generated income	$ 100,000
Net institutional support	$3,000,000

<u>Detailed Expenditures</u> are:

Personnel

University Library Administration			$125,000
General Administration			$100,000
Technical Services:	Library A	$230,000	
	Library B	25,000	
	Library C	80,000	$335,000
Reference (including ILL)			
	Library A	$320,000	
	Library B	$ 65,000	
	Library C	$110,000	$495,000
Circulation and Reserve			
	Library A	$125,000	
	Library B	$ 30,000	
	Library C	$ 40,000	$195,000
Special Services			
	Library A	$220,000	
	Library B	$ 10,000	
	Library C	$ 20,000	$250,000
Support Services			
	Library A	$100,000	
	Library B	25,000	
	Library C	25,000	$150,000

$1,650,000

<u>Support Expenditures</u>

General Office Costs $50,000

Automation Costs

Library A	$90,000		
Library B	$20,000		
Library C	$40,000	$150,000	
Travel and Staff Development		$ 30,000	
Equipment		$ 80,000	
Repairs and renovations		$ 80,000	
Telephone & Communications (Word Processor)		$ 50,000	
Maintenance Costs		$ 50,000	
Memberships		$ 10,000	$500,000

Library Resources

Library Materials:	Serials	$500,000		
	Books	$280,000		
	Other	$ 50,000		
	Binding	$ 70,000	$900,000	
Access Services:	ILL costs	$ 30,000		
	Computer costs	$ 20,000	50,000	$950,000

TOTAL:	$3,100,000

8

Total Resource Budget Planning for Academic Libraries

Sherman Hayes

Every generation of librarians is tempted to cry out against all of the new fiscal pressures on libraries. A reading of the historical literature seems to indicate that every generation has faced the same types of resource shortages and demands for new resources. This model of total resource budgeting recognizes that the source of the resource impacts significantly on the level and use of such resources.

In any given institutional budget process there are a number of budget projections being made simultaneously. The traditional operating budget request is produced using whatever criteria are demanded by the parent institution and it may be produced from the grass roots up or at the administrative level. The library administration, either systematically or casually, is meanwhile projecting a total resources budget. What limitations and directions of effort are dictated by the type of resources available? If the potential operating budget does not cover all of the needs, what other resources are available or need to be made available?

Much of this basic overview is common knowledge. This chapter is constructed using the following organization: statement of definitions and basic model; in-depth comments on resources and trends in each specific budget area; and implications in summary.

Total resource budget planning is a modeling framework which incorporates the techniques for identifying, enhancing, and documenting a wide variety of available resources. After identification, one can plan a program of enhancement or recognize the need for retrenchment. Then one designs a specific budget distribution system and control system for the available resources to accomplish library objectives.

The first plan, a total resource budget, is a plan which categorizes and identifies all potential resources available to accomplish the library's goals. Included in a total resource budget would be the traditional revenue provided by the parent institution in an *operating budget*. The operating budget is the normal annual revenue provided after the library presents to a higher administration a budget request describing needs and revenues requested to meet those needs. Most librarians are really referring to this budget when they talk of their budget increases or decreases or bemoan the lack of a sufficient budget. This is logical in that the operating budget, as contributed by the parent institution, is the primary budget. The two main components of library costs, labor and materials, are supported year after year by this basic commitment from the parent institution. For most institutions, the operating budgets reflects 60 to 70 percent of total resources available each year. Unfortunately, with the wide variety of resources used, but not reported, in standard library financial sources, the comparison of real budgets remains just an estimate.

A second revenue source that is a subset of total resource budget would be the *cash budget* which comes to the library independently of the primary operating budget process. This cash budget might include fees, endowments, cash gifts, auxiliary operations revenues, fines, and others. This revenue many times is not as predictable or steady as the primary budget but may be equally critical to the quality of the library.

The third resource available is in the *remainder budget* category of nonoperating, noncash budget acquired in support of goals and objectives. This would include contributed services, volunteers, certain gifts, and goodwill. In summary, then, a definition of a total resource budget might include: the operating budget, the cash budget, and the remainder budget. Fig-

Figure 8.1

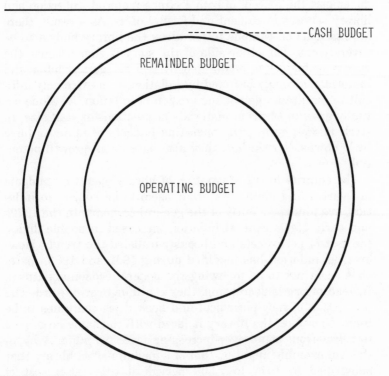

OPERATING BUDGET - Source: PARENT INSTITUTION

REMAINDER BUDGET - Source: CONTRIBUTED SERVICES, CERTAIN GIFTS, VOLUNTEERS, GOODWILL

CASH BUDGET   - Source: FEES, ENDOWMENTS, CASH GIFTS, AUXILIARY OPERATIONS, FINES

ure 8.1 conceptualizes the total resources available to a library.

OPERATING BUDGET

Most libraries have been hard pressed to maintain purchasing power from year to year with present operating budgets. The strength of the operating budget is also its weakness. That is, it represents the foundation or the basic cost of offering library service to a campus. Administration and faculty really do support the concept of both a strong materials collection and library services to student and faculty users. As a result, there is consensus on campus to not allow the library budget to be severely cut. The other side of the story is that because the operating budget is dominated by two categories, labor and materials, strongly buffeted by inflation, it is extremely difficult to maintain against the erosion of inflation, let alone actually grow in terms of materials acquisitions or staff size. In stock market terms, the operating budgets of libraries have little downside risk; but, they also have small growth potential.

The culprits in the stagnation of library operating budgets are varied and many. Materials seem to be subject to inflation, even independently of the general economy. In the 1970s and early 1980s general inflation increased in double digits; the cost of periodicals and books paralleled the trend.[1] However, as inflation has modified during 1982 and 1983, materials seem not to be following the general economic pattern. Instead of prices decreasing, they continue ever upward. The production of new periodical and book titles continues to be high. Therefore, the library is faced with the same large pool to select from at an ever-increasing price per item. A hypothetical example might be that of a medium-sized library that subscribed in 1977 to 2,500 periodical titles at a cost of $150,000. To maintain those same titles today would cost $306,450.[2]

The second major component of an operating budget is that of labor costs. A library is labor-intensive compared to many industries. Materials need to be prepared for use, services offered to assist and train in that use, and people to manage the checkout and return and other aspects of use. Over the last few years the perception of salary and how it is administered has been radically altered by severe inflation as represented by cost-of-living increases. Wage increases have become more an employee right than an incentive or merit for work performed. If the salary one earns needs to increase by 10 percent to just keep even, is it any wonder that significantly lower increases than that are perceived as inadequate. Fringe benefits have followed the same pattern. The Consumer Price Index for 1977 was 181.5 and for 1982 was 287.1.[3]

Another reason that the operating budget is difficult to increase radically is that it must go through several levels of competition for funding. Levels might include a college budget, a campus budget, a state board of education, and even a state legislative budget. This hierarchical competition makes it difficult to achieve great gains, in that a large gain means some other opportunity on campus or elsewhere is thwarted.

After this description of the sluggishness of operating budgets, one could become negative about operating budget growth potentials. There are, however, some areas where significant growth has been occurring.

The first one is in the area of automation. A large number of libraries have identified and added to their operating budget a third basic service leg called computer access. Expensive circulation systems and/or on-line catalogs have been added and maintained using general operating budgets. Perhaps the surest method of increasing an operating budget incrementally is to redefine the components, thus necessitating a major increase in funding. The discussion of operating budgets in the future will need to include labor, materials, and computing.

Three other techniques used on occasion to radically increase operating budgets are as follows. (1) A building expansion is used to increase staff, materials, and automation in an effort to meet the potential offered by the facility. More often, unfortunately, one gets the facility, together with greater expectations, but retains the same operating budget. (2) Another instance of potential growth occurs when a new type of material (information) is introduced or perfected. Examples in recent times would include microform, audiovisuals, and now microcomputer software. Many times the traditional users of periodicals and books join the library in advocating new funding for new material types to protect the level of spending for books and periodicals. (3) A third, and usually rare instance, is when the institution decides to completely upgrade the library in order to project the college or university at a new level of scholarly competence.

In summarizing the operating budget section, there are some

basic observations to be made: the narrowness of type of expenditures and basic size of the operating budget makes it difficult to increase this resource significantly. That same basic size also protects this funding source from fluctuations. Some other summary adjectives would include stable; structured; controlled; using local budget systems; predictable; and dominated by the big three expenditure categories of labor, materials, and computers.

CASH BUDGET

The cash budget consists of revenue which comes to the library independently of the operating budget process. Cash budgets in contrast to operating budgets are usually small, less controlled, more variable, and less predictable; yet they are critical to most libraries in maintaining an edge in accomplishment.

Cash gifts and endowments can supplement operating budgets, particularly in areas of collection enhancements. These resources often come with specific donor restrictions or guidelines imposed by the parent institution. The source of this revenue will frequently dictate usage.

Fines and costs retrieved for lost books are traditional sources of cash revenues. They are incidental revenue generated not for themselves but as enforcement tools in connection with usual circulation systems. Most fine systems are not self-supporting; in fact, if all such revenues go to a central nonlibrary fund, the enthusiasm for enforcement and collection is less than if funds come back to the library.

Fees for traditionally free library services or new services are becoming common. Typical of this category are interlibrary loan charges, search service fees, and library reproduction services, particularly if an audiovisual unit is attached to the library. Librarians seldom charge a full-payback rate for services. If one analyzes most fee-based charges for motive, one would find that they are imposed to control the growth of a new service or restrict the usage of an existing service. Interlibrary loan fees may be imposed knowing the main impact will be reduction in the usage of that service.

Grants do exist. After the heyday of the 1960s and early 1970s, one wonders if they are still available. Most grants impose almost as many budgetary control restrictions as the operating budget.

The last type of cash resources described here are those of auxiliary operations, operations which the library performs and does so as a cash generating center. They include services which help the patron or are needed in the library but are those that the library is glad to use to generate cash resources. Examples include: binding to the public, sign service, photocopiers, microfiche operations for other administrative units, various food or beverage vending options for the users, audiovisual rentals or services to other campus units, other copying services, and many more.

The revenues from these are often used to support the actual costs of the service. Profits, if any, revert to other library operations. Perhaps the most effective use of auxiliary services receipts is for budget transfer purposes. For example, revenues from a photocopier are placed in a fund. The machine costs, supplies, and paper are charged to this fund. Any excess cash becomes available for the total resource budget planning process. Note, however, that staff labor to monitor the machine, make change, and replace paper and chemicals is probably absorbed into the duties of those paid with the operating budget. The library therefore reduces the potential operating budget efficiency and transfers it to the cash revenue side. This is done mainly because the accounting becomes burdensome and it is difficult to identify, exactly, staff contributions to auxiliary enterprises. In reality, this type of transfer is not increasing resources, but changing the type of resource. As a result, the library may have more flexibility in using cash resources versus operating budget.

Another attribute of cash budgets is that they often remain available to you over a changing fiscal year; that is, they do not revert to a general fund under someone else's control as do most operating budget general balances.

Cash resources may become the fund that can move your library forward, such as being used for staff development, or a special purchase. This budget resource needs to be identified, protected, and enlarged whenever possible.

REMAINDER BUDGET

Recently, an in-depth case study was conducted at the University of North Dakota library to determine what services and items were contributed to the library in addition to the operating budget, but which were not identified as part of that budget. These contributed services represented a 40 percent addition in value to the operating budget.[4] In planning a total resource budget, librarians need to recognize the contributed services from units in the parent institution as well as volunteers, gifts, and goodwill.

Most libraries operate within a larger institution that, in turn, offers centralized services to each unit. Examples include: personnel, purchasing, physical plant, building cleaning and maintenance, and computer services; work-study funding; affirmative action efforts; duplicating or printing; parking; utilities; mail services; and accounting.

Many times the other resource sources of operating and cash budgets cannot be used to meet needs. Librarians need to effectively include contributed services as a potential resource. Perhaps an example would help. Recently our university has been attempting to integrate the microcomputer into the academic support system for students and faculty and we at the library have been struggling to define our role in this new information area. The computer center and academic planning committees had equipment funds available. They approached us to place a center containing 15 microcomputers in the library. We offered space, furniture (used and in storage), software, and circulation services. We made initial purchases of basic software packages while specialized packages came from departmental book funds at faculty requests. The computer center services the machines; we assist the user in circulation and general usage of software packages. Although our materials budget did not increase, faculty can now choose to purchase software if they feel it is more effective than book purchases. Our operating budget did not support the acquisition of $50,000 worth of microcomputers, but by using contributed services (equipment and expertise) we now offer a service we feel is critical to the library and academic community.

Contributed services are affected greatly by the general health of the overall institutional budget. When times are good, we all seem to be more generous. When times are tight, then contributed services come under pressure. Recently our plant services unit had its budget for maintenance and improvements to facilities cut severely. As a result, small projects such as changing a door lock, previously offered free, are now charged back to our budgets. If others are contributing the service, you generally play by their rules. Just as one is attempting to increase this resource by getting another unit to "contribute" assistance, remember others are looking to the library to help as a "contributor."

Volunteers and contributed salary funds, such as work-study, represent labor made available outside the operating budget. The source is less stable than operating budget salaries (witness the CETA program) and particularly in the use of volunteers. Further, operating budget resources are generally used to maintain control and gain efficient results from this source.

Many physical items are donated to libraries. The common ones are books and manuscript collections. As with most contributed services categories, operating budget resources are needed to judge the quality of physical gifts and to integrate them into the collections. If these resources are honestly assessed, planned for, and incorporated into the total resource picture, they can be invaluable; when they are not anticipated or when one cannot make operating budget resources available for control, they often fail.

The last component discussed in the noncash budget category is goodwill. Goodwill is a balance sheet dollar figure used in profit-making corporations or businesses. In selling a business, goodwill is actually negotiated as having a monetary value. Some descriptors would include name recognition, general community attitudes toward the company, and other measurements of the subjective value the enterprise brings to bear in addition to inventory, services, and staff. Since libraries do not have a balance sheet, the goodwill concept is not frequently used, yet it is a valid resource in total resource budgeting to document, subjectively measure, and use. Edward R. Johnson in a recent article cited seven general responses to a questionnaire on coping in the 1980s.[5] The most frequent coping technique listed was *Politics*. Johnson and the respondents to his survey are really describing the real life process of developing goodwill. You need to establish the library in the minds of faculty and administration as a positive, helpful, visible force on campus.

Before instituting any major service or collection expansion, you should identify allies and supporters on campus. Recognize that in your total resource budget, goodwill is a valuable commodity which needs constant replenishment and planned usage.

The overall category of noncash, nonoperating budgets can be described as widely variable between institutions, as it hinges on skills of library staff which are, to a great extent, difficult to document and account for. It represents a great potential for small and large growth in library resources.

SUMMARY

Although the pressures to find adequate resources are constant, generation to generation, there are different emphases for tomorrow than for yesterday. Factors which impact most significantly on total resource budgeting in the late 1980s are as follows.

1. Automation is a new, complicated, and costly service which needs to be funded in the *operating budget*.

2. With shrinking college enrollments and inflationary salary pressures, new staff is not a likely alternative. Innovative librarians will therefore concentrate on increasing their *operating budget's* efficiency not just their size.

3. With the reduction in available grant money, the *cash budget* sources most likely to increase will be auxiliary enterprises and fees charged for services offered.

4. As most institutions of higher education consolidate in the 1980s, the skills necessary for acquiring the library's fair share of stagnant or shrinking resource will be taxed. In acquiring remainder budget resources, the librarian will need to build strong political goodwill and have a large number of contributed services to maintain quality and improve upon the status quo.

NOTES

1. Chandler B. Grannis, "U.S. Title Output Average Prices: Final Figures for 1982," *Publishers Weekly* 224 (13) (Sept. 23, 1983): 29–32.

2. Norman B. Brown and Jane Phillips, "Price Indexes for 1983: U.S. Periodicals and Serial Services," *Library Journal* 108 (15) (Sept. 1, 1983) 1659–62.

3. U.S. Department of Commerce, Bureau of the Census 1982–1983, *Statistical Abstract of the United States* (Washington, D.C.: Government Printing Office).

4. Sherman Hayes, "What Does It Really Cost to Run Your Library?" *Journal of Library Administration* 1 (2) (Summer 1980): 1–10.

5. Edward R. Johnson, "Financial Planning Needs of Publicly-Supported Academic Libraries in the 1980s: Politics as Usual," *Journal of Library Administration* 3 (3/4) (Fall/Winter 1982): 23–36.

III

NEW OPPORTUNITIES

9

Library Automation and Economics in a Period of Rapidly Changing Technology: Two Perspectives

Richard W. McCoy and David C. Weber

Stanford University became a member of the Research Libraries Group (RLG) in 1978, and thus joined with other institutions to develop cooperative programs in collection development, preservation, and the enhancement of shared access to library materials. Since many program elements require a common data base and automated systems, the RLG undertook the transformation of the former Stanford BALLOTS system into the Research Libraries Information Network (RLIN). It became the technical base for the support of the programs of the RLG partnership.

Constant advances in technology offer choices for research libraries and create new imperatives for service to scholars. At the same time funds for library improvements are in very short supply. Some of the technological choices present major economic and management challenges.

This chapter explores some of the salient features of current technical change and related economic challenges from two perspectives: that of an institution committed to cooperative action and challenged by the need to fulfill rapidly increasing user expectations in times of scarce resources, and that of a partnership seeking to build and sustain efforts to solve problems and exploit opportunities which can best be addressed in a cooperative environment. While the situation is described in a particular context, it is representative of the challenges librarians in general must face.

THE TECHNOLOGY

The pace of technological development is rapid and shows no sign of slowing. Many observers see in the new technologies forces which will change the face of higher education. Individual institutions are assigning responsibility for meeting this challenge to officers more senior in the academic structure and are addressing with some urgency the changes they will bring.

There are many exciting technological developments which will both support and challenge academic and research libraries. Three major elements influencing the changes in which libraries will participate are presented here to establish a common context.

1. High band width communications and digital communications nets are being installed at a fast pace. Local area networks will allow quick access to resources and will soon terminate in most offices as phone lines do now. Library bibliographic resources will be among the most useful and sought after resources on these networks. Wide area networks must develop rapidly to keep pace. In this context, the Linked Systems Project of RLG, the Washington Library Network (WLN) and the Library of Congress (LC) are applying international standards to the interconnection of major library networks and work is already begun on using the same linkage technology to communicate with local library systems.

    Consequences: Interconnectivity will enhance the prospects for sharing of resources and for a new national shared cataloging activity; a "logical" national library network and data base can exist where many obstacles would prevent achieving a physical network; local library systems will reside concurrently on local area and wide area networks, and through "gateways" will access other less frequently used resources; reference searching can proceed from local resources to national, and then to the great libraries of Europe and other parts of the world.

2. Personal computers are becoming ubiquitous features of faculty offices and studies. There are 16 machines in the offices of the

Stanford libraries and about a third of the RLG staff members now have them. Personal computers are gaining in power and function too. Early in the next decade, computers may be found wherever a campus telephone is today and some of these will be extremely powerful scholar work stations.

Consequences: Many of the effects which these machines will have by the end of this decade cannot be forecast by extrapolation of today's experiences; the changes we are experiencing are qualitative and revolutionary. Bibliographic and text files will be down loaded, maintained as local data bases, and incorporated into the process of research and authorship. Integration of national data bases, local library systems, and individual work stations into a continuous seamless model will be possible. The process of reaching out from a work station to campus or national and international resources will not produce the abrupt transitions we experience today which may require us to log on and off and switch among complex protocols.

3. Mass storage costs will continue to fall and storage densities will increase. Optical disks now appearing as video playback media and making a challenge for the LP record market will become a common medium for storing digital data. Magnetic storage vendors will also deliver new ultra-high-density products into the market.

Consequences: Local library systems will be able to store data bases of the size of the large union data bases now found only at central sites (9 gigabytes at OCLC, Inc., 10 gigabytes at the Library of Congress, 18 gigabytes at RLG and all growing). Full text storage will become affordable when we solve the problems of copyright and related financial interests. Optical disks may well emerge as a data base distribution medium, with the equivalent of the RLIN data base or the National Union Catalog (NUC) updated once each week and delivered to your institution in a small package. Optical storage media will also become available as an alternative to microfilm for preservation.

These three ingredients in technological change create imperatives for action which cannot be ignored. They create the challenges and opportunities which will strain individual institutions and cooperative efforts alike.

Local integrated library systems meeting local needs and doing much of what is now being done on networks (E.g., RLIN,

OCLC and WLN) will become available, affordable, and necessary tools of academic and research libraries. Component systems are available today and integration is beginning to develop. Rich searching of large data bases will be affordable even on local systems. With the emergence of highly capable local systems, we will no longer require group commitment to cooperative networks to obtain technical processing services, though we will still require, of course, access to shared data.

THE ECONOMICS

Universities, libraries, and automated systems are strongly affected by budgetary capacities and limitations. Libraries almost always lack venture capital or funds for research and development, and they commonly find it difficult to obtain funds for qualitative improvements. Libraries generally need one to three years from the point when an automated system is desired until it is in place and up to projected production. The reallocation of library funds from staff to automation services, either purchased from a utility or developed on an in-house system, is only sometimes a cost savings or a tradeoff; automated alternatives have frequently resulted in a net increase in budget. Academic officers are more realistic now than 15 or 20 years ago when many viewed automation merely as a budget cutting prospect.

Despite the fact that technology costs and equipment price performance are rapidly improving, library automation costs have not come down rapidly on a unit transaction basis in part because personnel costs are an increasing percentage of system costs. The need to maintain systems and the desire to upgrade, add to, or change to more cost-effective hardware all require highly skilled and expensive personnel. (Hardware, once 75–85 percent of system costs is now 35–45 percent, and decreasing as a percentage of the whole.) The effective life of system hardware and software is relatively short—five or six years for a major computer, the same for basic software, frequently three to five years for terminals, and two to four years for versions of an application system. In the next decade or two, hardware costs will continue to drop, staff costs will tend to normalize, and software, we hope, will have increasingly useful life spans.

In the near term, justification for the purchase of automated systems can come only in part from direct labor savings. The rest must come from such qualitative improvements as timeliness, more effective bibliographic searching, simultaneous and distance-independent access, a degree of improved accuracy, and similar value gains from system linkages. Society at large, and educational institutions in their internal budgeting and goal-setting processes, must determine how much those improvements are wanted, and at what rate of progress they should be implemented.

THE INSTITUTIONAL PERSPECTIVE

Planning must start with an administrative philosophy. At the Stanford University Libraries, the philosophy is to use automation only where it is cost effective or where it provides significant service improvements for faculty and students. The libraries have not sought to be far ahead of the requirements of the faculty or of the university. Since first introducing automated systems in 1963, they have used state-of-the-art, exclusively off-the-shelf equipment, but have sought to improve applications. The university is strong, however, in computer science, mathematics, engineering, operations research, and business, so the environment is particularly conducive to library automation.

The libraries have set as automation goals: ordering and cataloging all library materials in all languages; support of public access and national links for access to this same range and form of research resources; all reasonable use of commercial indexing and abstracting services; a minimum of costs passed on to library users; public information on the specific current location of all materials; coordinated support for access to quantitative as well as textual data sets and acquisition of all such materials which fall within the library acquisition policy. A further goal is full integration with other campus information resources needed for scholarship. Participation in a coordinated academic data program is a prime example. The libraries also intend to support all cost effective administrative automation.

Stanford falls short of these goals at present. It lacks, for example, automated support for Arabic, Hebraic, and Cyrillic, though, except for the acquisition function, it now has that support for Chinese, Japanese, and Korean. Retrospective conversion of paper records has hardly begun. Circulation and serial piece receipt control is lacking. National linkages are, as yet, primitive. High speed, low cost, remote digital facsimile transmission is lacking and administrative automation is limited. It is financial capacity, not technology, which has governed the Stanford rate of progress. It is ongoing operational cost which has been a dominant concern, although one-time expense can be formidable, as with retrospective conversion for example.

"How to afford it?" Is the key question, followed by the related "What costs, if any, should be passed on to others?" Three examples will show the necessarily pragmatic approaches taken.

1. Commercial indexing services, such as Dialog, have been offered by the libraries for over a decade. While continuing costs for staff and hardware have been absorbed, the incremental costs incurred in answering a patron request have been charged to the user, except when the library staff member has chosen to use the commercial service as the most cost effective means to respond. Stanford is currently experimenting with Sci-Mate for direct user searching and may experiment with the use of charged student-intermediary "stringers" as means of controlling the amount of staff time going into this service, thereby transferring some effort back to some users.

2. A public on-line catalog exists on a Stanford local area network. It is named Socrates (for its Socratic interactive questioning to elicit precise and useful responses). Socrates has provided at Stanford a natural response to the free-vs.-fee dilemma. Socrates terminals in library units are fully budgeted and available during all hours the libraries are open. Library patrons have open free access, just as they have had to card catalogs. Socrates has also taken its place as a resource on the campus computing network in which the practice has long been established of patron payment for units of

service used. Home and office users of Socrates pay for this resource in the same manner they would for any of the many other services of the network. Value decisions made by users thus lead to a source of funds to support the added costs of wide access to the catalog.

3. Academic data sets of textual or quantitative information (E.g., census data) present a different situation. In this case, the libraries buy and catalog data sets which meet book selection policy criteria; the data are kept in the campus computing center where the cost of use is charged to the requestor. Library reference staff members guide patrons in the use of code books and advantageous printed sources which complement or supplement the machine-readable data. University funds for research and instructional use of the computing center are allocated to schools and academic departments, which in turn may allocate these funds for use of such data sets if they choose. Incidentally, such funds may also be used for lab, office, or home use of Socrates, since that service is supplied by the same computing center. Efforts are now being made to offer commercial indexing and other data services via the computing center network, so as to consolidate billing, encourage direct faculty access, and gain bulk rate advantages.

In order to describe the affect on library automation expenses we must first define automation costs. Stanford Libraries include in this category, contractual services (such as those of RLIN, and Dialog), equipment and telecommunications, expenses against grants for automation studies or development, and in-house programming staff costs. Given that definition, the libraries in 1982–83 spent 5.03 percent of their expenditures on automation. In 1980–81 it was 3.97 percent and in 1981–82 at 4.07 percent; in 1983–84 it is projected at 5.49 percent. During these same years technical processing staff costs rose in relation to automation costs (the former rose from 75 to 79 percent of the total; automation thus dropped from 25 to 21 percent even though expenditures increased) and this trend has continued over the past eight years even during periods when the automated functions and the number of personnel have remained constant.

As an aside, Stanford's 5.5 percent of total expenditures for automation is not excessive. Rough percentage figures for other universities are: 2.5 at Rice, 3.9 at Harvard, 4.9 at Pennsylvania, 5.0 at Yale, 5.2 at Texas, 6.0 at UCLA, 6.6 at Michigan, 6.7 at Columbia, 7.0 at Brigham Young, 7.1 at Cornell, 7.2 at Berkeley, and 7.8 at Chicago.

Of the 5.49 percent Stanford budgeted this year for equipment and contractual services, the breakdown is:

General services (training, maintenance, and communications)	38%
RLIN technical service support	44%
RLIN public service support	4%
Data services by public services staff	5%
Computing center services	9%

The direct costs to Stanford are obviously substantial. Further, almost every library function and every organizational unit uses terminals. More than one hundred terminals exist in processing and service locations, in business and administrative offices, and in book selection curatorial offices. As a consequence, automation has resulted in an upgrading of support staff skills, revised classification assignments and increased salary scales for support staff. This degree of automation and consequent salary shift and budgetary consequences should be expected when a major program of on-line library automation is implemented.

There is conviction at Stanford that, first, given the limited funds available, academic and other research libraries can only maximize the advance of scholarly support through joint effort. Second, performance gains are quite immediate and apparent; cost savings over manual processes materialize more slowly, and projects may in fact take a decade or so to prove their worth on a solely financial basis. Third, there are attitudinal, even spiritual, benefits to the library staff from a serious joint effort among major institutions, supported by presidents and trustees. Staff concerns for the collections, services, and personnel of other institutions are matters of great personal interest, and indeed local self-interest; what happens elsewhere will directly affect local library effectiveness. Fourth, grants to the Research Libraries Group flow through to its member institutions. Thus, new RLG systems have been developed at no direct costs to members, and preservation initiatives and retrospective conversion steps in member libraries, for example, have been partially funded by grants to RLG. This too is part of the benefit which accrues to Stanford through the research support partnership. The sum of the individual actions is clearly greater than the parts. The financial investment is large, but essential and appropriate to the intellectual benefits which are widespread and far-reaching.

There are risks as well in this automation effort. While the Stanford Libraries believe they were wise not to create an in-house programming staff, they are therefore dependent on the rate of progress provided by others. Product stability has been enhanced, yet accurate multiyear forecasting of schedules and costs is made more difficult. Commercial component integration seems sometimes more complex. There is heavy dependence on both the campus computing facility and on RLG, and the library automation budget is determined in that larger context. Naturally, there would be risks in any alternative scenario as well. Only in the historic perspective of what 10 or 20 years have provided for students, faculty, and research staff can a final grade be given as to Stanford's success of applying technology for scholarly gain.

THE CONSORTIUM PERSPECTIVE

The Research Libraries Information Network has just been brought to state-of-the-art technical status and economically self-sufficient operation. It continues to gain program support capabilities at high pace. Today's archival and manuscript control will be followed by control over museum objects; Chinese, Japanese and Korean (CJK) will be followed by support for other non-Roman scripts. Preservation, collection management, and shared resources all enjoy support recently added or planned for early enhancement. These accomplishments are very recent indeed, many completed within the last half year.

Technical and economic factors described above have prompted a transition which will challenge the partnership, change the technical nature of RLIN and require a major overhaul in the way in which shared programs are supported economically. The management of this transition will be the critical challenge of the next years. RLG knows a good deal about the plans of members and will work with them in a co-ordinated move toward a distributed environment in which much of the technical processing now done on RLIN will be best done locally, in which the total holdings of all users will be in a shared data base, and all programs will continue to be supported.

There are several factors which greatly complicate the distributed transition. (1) Our members will clearly not select a single technical system for local use; there will be several, though we will work hard to avoid maximizing diversity. (2) They will not be moving on the same time schedule toward local systems; some expect *and desire* to be well behind the leaders (in time frame). RLIN must support the complexity of multiple local system types, and maintain for several years a central technical processing service for what could be a less than economical volume of activity.

A special challenge follows from the very extensive program support capabilities in RLIN, which do not exist in any of the emerging candidates for local system use. It does not seem attractive to support these special capabilities centrally while bread-and-butter work is done on local systems. But these are precisely the features which must survive the technological transition.

So, what will we do when cataloging goes away? RLIN's role will change from that of a shared and centralized technical processing system to that of a data resource node in an interconnected network of research library systems. The ground work was laid long ago in work leading to the Linked System Project and designed to connect diverse systems. Work is now proceeding with several builders of local systems toward implementing the same link which now connects RLIN with the Washington Library Network (WLN) and the Library of Congress. Further, we plan for RLIN itself to become an exportable system available to organizations with like objectives. Plans are being made, as well, for the changes in the RLIN data base which distribution will require. When local systems carry complete bibliographic records and take their place as part of a truly distributed data base environment, then the library-specific records now in RLIN will be replaced by references to their local counterparts.

The RLIN we see for the future will service local systems with the data which they require from other than local sources. It will provide the means of sharing program support data for collection development, preservation and the sharing of resources, and it will serve to support the hierarchical extension of reference searching from local to national and to international resources. Fortunately, RLIN was designed from the start as a public service tool; with subject searching, boolean searching, and 29 indexes to locate material even when only partial information is available. Its extensive searching capabilities were designed for effective reference and public service use. Operating within an expanded linked systems environment, RLIN will contribute its share to a logical national network supporting open sharing of bibliographic records.

It is important to differentiate *distribution* from decentralization or from stand-alone local systems. The differences are critical and failing to keep them in focus could be a fatal error for a consortium like the Research Libraries Group and we are convinced it would be a serious mistake for individual libraries. Essential characteristics of a distributed system must include the ability to continue to interact with a shared data base (even though it may not be physically in one place), the retention of the program support functions we have enjoyed in a centralized system, and full linkage between participating nodes and functions.

THE COSTS OF COOPERATION

While the most difficult challenges facing research libraries in collection development, preservation, and retrospective conversion can best be addressed in a shared environment, cooperation is not necessarily easy, nor is it free.

Most members of the RLG consortium have invested significant amounts of capital in the building of RLIN, and numerous foundation grants have also been applied. While these investments can be attributed in part to the costs of doing routine technical processing, much was applied in support of cooperative programs which are the heart of the RLG effort. Transaction fees for RLIN users are higher than those of OCLC or WLN users. The difference is offset by added functional capacity, but a part of this cost could be attributed to cooperative programs as well. Board members now travel to four meetings and several staff members from each institution travel to two committee meetings annually. These travel costs are also a cost of cooperation.

In the cooperative process, it has sometimes been frustrating to see how long it takes, first to agree on the nature of an attack on a problem, and then to see it fully implemented. CJK, the Conspectus, Archives and Manuscripts, the Linked System Project all have required enormous effort, patience and determination. These are also cost factors in cooperation and part of the price of supporting exceptional research libraries.

Finally, consortium members have from time to time, deferred local plans or made choices not locally optimal in order to provide for continued viability of the consortium. In the move toward distribution, there will certainly be more choices of this kind.

THE BENEFITS OF COOPERATION

In the work being accomplished, it is very difficult to measure program benefits in quantitative terms. The cost side of the equation (or at least the major components) can be easily added, but how are the value of program accomplishments measured?

The conspectus, primary collecting responsibilities (an endangered species list for research collections), and the choices in acquisition decisions identify a major cost benefit target of partnership effort; it enables long-term dollar savings in acquisitions, or the production of a greater value from scarce resources. The information we now have is largely anecdotal, but we believe we are on the threshold of producing a major and essential return, essential because of the budget cuts and purchasing power erosion we have already experienced.

What will be the value of preserving American imprints of

the last quarter of the nineteenth century? Priceless perhaps. What is the significance of a shared network already linking almost all major East Asian collections, and changing qualitatively the support for this area of scholarship? What will be the effect and the value of combining into a common search environment archival, manuscript, and museum material joining traditional library resources? And what of the bridges established between universities, independent research libraries, and museums? We remain convinced that these and other program steps will return a value many times the dollars invested. On this intellectual balance sheet we recognize that the support of advanced tools of scholarship is not inexpensive.

Let us suggest two other benefits which, like the conspectus which has been adopted by Association of Research Libraries (ARL), may produce a broad benefit for all academic libraries whether or not a part of our particular group. First, the Linked Systems Project with LC and WLN needed this combination of three participants to demonstrate its generality and to provide an initial mix likely to lead to expansion. This and follow-on activity will be important ingredients in assuring the continued open sharing of bibliographic records, in bringing about a new national shared cataloging program. It will establish the basis for a "logical" national network and for the interconnection of local library systems. We believe that most major academic libraries will be in networks linked by this technology in the not distant future. Second, it is also likely that the efforts of this "impatient" RLG membership group, wanting early progress and desiring special capabilities, serve as a model and sometimes an irritant. To the extent that encourages other networks and individual institutions to move more rapidly in related directions, we believe it is another benefit of cooperation.

EXAMPLES FROM STANFORD/RLG EXPERIENCE

The Socrates development serves as a good example of the coincidence of local and consortium goals. RLG supplied more than one million full Machine Readable Cataloging (MARC) records of Stanford holdings to load the catalog and now provides regular updates. A search of Socrates in many cases may be followed by a search of RLIN (now with reference librarian assistance) in an initial example of the referred searching which we expect will soon be facilitated by intersystem linkage.

While Socrates provides an example of coincident priorities, acquisitions is an example to the contrary and one in which current discussion is underway between Stanford and RLG. Stanford has for ten years been a user of the RLIN acquisition system and thus contributes its data to the collection development program. Stanford has considered selecting acquisitions as one of the next activities to support on a local system and would be prepared to load the resulting data onto RLIN and to share it through intersystem linkages when available. These steps would provide for continued support of collection management program objectives. The idiosyncratic and non-MARC format of the acquisition records produced by stand-alone systems makes them unlikely candidates for batch loading, and intersystem linkage priorities are being set in ways that make early connection to a stand-alone acquisition processor unlikely.

This then is an example of inconsistent priorities. A decision is required and will be made with consultation between both interested parties; the choice made will not only have a technical result but also shift economic burden. For Stanford, internally, the decision must also be made in consideration of how a local acquisition system might become a part of its future integrated capabilities.

These are two recent examples of the kinds of technical and economic choices which follow from cooperative efforts in a period of rapid change.

We have presented two perspectives of the same forces and events which are affecting us all. The challenges from these two viewpoints are quite different and the opportunities are sometimes independent. The need to meet local service requirements when combined with budget constraints may dictate a pace of action difficult to adjust to in a shared environment which must also deal with considerable local diversity.

Given the needs of faculty, advanced students, research staff, and scholars in general, however, we share a conviction that the major problems of research libraries can best be solved in a shared environment. The mission of supporting advanced scholarship requires cooperation of those bearing responsibility for the nation's research institutions through this challenging period of rapid technological and economic transition.

10

Networks

Jo An S. Segal

DEFINITIONS

There are several definitions of networks which have led many times to serious confusion over the meaning of the word. First of all we have an informal definition of something often referred to as networking, which simply means knowing who knows what and linking up with them in some way. As one special librarian said to me at one time, a library in a network is a library with connections and we all need connections. It was this sense of connection which Carol Niemeyer stressed in the theme for her year as American Library Association (ALA) president.

Cooperative activities among libraries have existed for many years at a variety of levels from a small consortium of libraries sharing information about interlibrary loans, purchasing cooperatives, processing centers, regional systems within states, state library networking activities, multitype and multistate organizations, and even national ones. Using the term "network" for all of these entities can lead to confusion and a fear of competition, which will be addressed later in the section called Levels of Networking, and which looms as a real danger to the promulgation of cooperative activities among libraries.

The proliferation of the term network has ironically led to removing that name from the organizations most deserving of it, and dubbing them instead with the strange title of "bibliographic utilities." The concept of a utility as a monopolistic enterprise providing services without which life cannot continue and often seeming heartless and cruel is not one which is cherished by those who manage such utilities.

Although the term network has been applied to all kinds of organizations of libraries, the topic of this chapter is a certain kind of network which provides services to its members largely in the field of cooperation and automation, which usually involve actual telecommunications links between the libraries and some host computer containing the data the libraries need.

COOPERATION IS GOOD

Since we have now embarked on 1984, I think it might be well for us to adopt a slogan. Library cooperation has a long history dating from Jewett's 1853 proposal for a National Union Catalog and running through several versions of interlibrary loan codes, several kinds of union lists of serials and newspapers, cooperative processing centers, shared cataloging, and most recently clustered circulation systems and on-line public access catalogs.

At the macro level one has seen the development of several very large networks providing shared cataloging and other automated technical services to libraries of all types and sizes. These networks include OCLC, RLIN, WLN, and University of Toronto Library Automation System (UTLAS). They have all developed over the last 15 years. All have very large data bases and provide high quality technical service systems for libraries based on the MARC format. The recent development of micro or personal computers has tended to alter somewhat the perception that cooperation is good. Many libraries feel that the smaller computers allow them to carry out operations individually which they formerly could do only through cooperative enterprises. But abandoning the cooperative mode will probably be regretted in the long run, as the libraries find an ongoing need to identify bibliographic information with a minimum of duplicative effort, and to be able to share with one another on a broad geographical basis. However, the micro-computers and the powerful minicomputers which have been developed enable libraries to develop secondary products, such as on-line catalogs and circulation systems which are effective at the individual institution level or at the level of clusters of institutions. These mini-cooperative projects are an extremely valuable result of recent technological development.

GOVERNANCE

Writing in 1977 for a national seminar on Networks for Networkers, Carlile defined governance as, "the structure and administration of the power relationships among the various organizational stakeholders [members or constituents] within the shared activity or network." as opposed to management, "the operational process by which resources are obtained and used to accomplish the organizational objectives set by the governance." It is up to the governance board to set the mission goals and objectives of the organization at the macro level. These goals are then carried out by the staff.

There are three basic types of network organization. The first is governmental, that is, the network is part of some other governmental agency. For example, FEDLINK, the network which provides automated services to federal libraries throughout the country, appears on the organizational chart of the Library of Congress. ILLINET and NEBASE are oper-ated as part of the state library agencies in Illinois and Ne-braska. INCOLSA is a separate agency funded by the State of Indiana. MINITEX is governed by the Minnesota Higher Ed-ucation Coordinating Board, and SUNY/OCLC is part of the State University of New York. Although their specific govern-ing authorities differ, all of these networks are governmental agencies and their governance structures are determined by the laws of their states.

It would be possible to have a network set up as a quasi-governmental agency, but none of the networks now providing OCLC services falls into this category.

Most frequently, the agencies known as networks are not-for-profit corporations of various sizes. Among this type of organization are networks which serve single states, or relatively small regions, such as CAPCON, MLC, MLNC, OHIONET, PRLC, and WILS. Five networks which serve rather large multistate regions are AMIGOS, BCR, NELINET, PALINET, and SOLINET. The advantages of the not-for-profit membership corporation, according to Carlile, are as follows.

1. It is easy to create.
2. It is a separate legal entity.
3. It allows central management of the network at the network level.
4. It provides continuity of existence.
5. Its liability is limited by the legal constraints on the corporation.
6. It enjoys a favorable tax structure.
7. The flexibility of organizational form, purpose, powers, and governance are of great advantage to the members.

Governance boards vary from network to network. BCR has a governance board consisting of 14 members. Six of them serve by virtue of their office as the chief officer of the state library agency in the six primary member states: Colorado, Iowa, Kansas, South Dakota, Utah, and Wyoming. The other eight trustees are elected by BCR members as follows: five are elected by constituents according to type of library; one each from research libraries, academic libraries, public libraries, special libraries, and schools and processing centers. Three are elected at large by all the members. This means that all librarians in the BCR region are represented on the board according to geography by their state library, according to type of library level by their type-of-library representative trustee, and generally by three individuals who represent the entire constituency.

LEVELS OF NETWORKING

There are implicit levels of networking. These are of several sorts: type-of-library networks, size-of-library networks, and geographical-area networks at various aggregations of area: local, substate region, state, multistate, and national.

As one thinks about cooperation among libraries, it doesn't take much effort to realize that certain activities are appropriately carried out at certain levels. For instance, clustered on-line public access catalogs are probably most appropriate at a relatively small geographical area, and perhaps among same-type libraries, while interlibrary loan networks probably benefit from a very large and widespread base of holdings information—thus, at the national level.

For years, the library literature in this country discussed the national network, the emerging national network, and even the *de facto* national network. There was a sort of manifest destiny concept which pointed in the direction of a single, coordinated network at the national level. However, librarians balked at the idea. They feared the imposition of authority from a pyramidal or hierarchical authority. The idea of a single national network is weakening.

Nevertheless, a key aspect of the levels-of-networking concept is to define as clearly as possible the purpose of networking activity and the optimum level for carrying out the activity. This will avoid some of the mindless fear of the threat of competition. As soon as any organization arises which can possibly be called a network from any perspective, we are warned that it may pose a threat to some other cooperative enterprise. Clarity of purpose and mission will allow a variety of networks to work together in the service of libraries. One library may find itself in several overlapping networks for a variety of purposes. It may belong to an institution which is part of an academic consortium, thus sharing some library activities with sister institutions. It may be part of a group contract for data base searching activity. It may be a member of OCLC and/or RLIN; a part of a regional library system which offers courier delivery; party to a joint on-line catalog with other institutions; and a participant in an interlibrary loan program run by its state library. The problem is to find a way to link these networks so that the library is best served.

PROGRAM DEVELOPMENT

It is this sense of service to the library members of networks which drives the development of programs to be offered by networks. A combination of informed judgment by board and staff, coupled with market research efforts to determine librarians' desires and potential use of products and services leads to a mix of network offerings. For a network like BCR, which desires to offer full service, such marketing work is indispensable.

Steps in program development include:

1. planning—development of long-range and shorter-term plans setting the framework for network activity

2. situational analysis—study of external environmental conditions affecting the organization, its members, the market in general, the competition, and the like

3. needs assessment—a study of the needs, wants, and desires of the members and other potential target markets

4. cost analysis—a study of the cost of providing a service, including cost of product, staffing, overhead, and possible ways to recover the costs

For example, the BCR Long Range Planning Committee is in the process of revising the organization's long-term goals. It has drafted a mission statement and staff has carried out a situational analysis. By the end of the fiscal year, a multiyear planning document will be adopted by the board to guide the organization in its program development.

MARKETING AND USER SERVICES

The concept of marketing network products and services seems to some to be at odds with the idea of selecting programs needed and wanted by libraries. Yet it is in the effective marketing of services that networks provide leadership to libraries, encouraging them to innovate, to try new methods, to test out new technologies. Effective marketing also tends to reduce costs to each user, in that bulk purchasing of services by networks results in reduced unit costs to members.

Also implicit in the concept of marketing is the idea of keeping members satisfied by means of member service activities. User members need to be able to call on network staff for help, technical assistance, and advice. Staff must visit libraries, call librarians frequently on the telephone, anticipate member needs, and be responsive to member complaints, both direct and indirect.

It is perfectly reasonable for a network to set marketing and service goals for at least one year in advance and to monitor attainment of those goals. Methods for marketing include demonstrations at network offices, in various sites throughout network territory, and at library conferences. Introductory training sessions to familiarize members with a service, allowing some time for free use, may allow a service to sell itself. Letters pointing out advantages of a service or product may be sent to all members, or only to a segment identified as a good potential target market (e.g., System Development Corporation (SDC) services aimed at petroleum libraries). Articles in the newsletter of the network or of the target market and advertising may be effective.

In the past, networks have largely been reactive in marketing. They have waited to be approached by potential users; then only have they reacted positively with information, demonstrations, and so forth. Recently, more networks are taking a more proactive stance, recognizing the advantages to all members of larger group contracts and shared system use.

Communication with members is an integral part of marketing and user services. Such devices as a general newsletter sent to an audience larger than the membership are useful in attracting potential network members and in conveying general information about networking as a whole, about specific interests of all network members, and about the particular network. Technical memoranda provide users of certain technical systems with valuable updated information on system developments, usage, and answers to questions. Information bulletins are sometimes needed to give members timely information about important network developments affecting them, such as prices, contracts, or telecommunications developments. Open meetings at state library conferences, for instance, give members a chance to get information and to communicate their needs. Site visits—by staff to libraries and by member librarians to headquarters—are one of the most valuable means of communication in the network.

Training sessions also provide a unique communication opportunity for the trainer to answer questions about the network and its services, while observing firsthand what is going on in the member library environment and learning about member librarians and their needs.

Technical assistance is the most common service provided to users. Network staff must have the expertise necessary to provide such assistance and the communication skills required to elicit positive responses from users.

FINANCING OF NETWORKS

One of the problems with financing networks or any other library related activity is the psychology which many librarians have regarding how things are paid for. There is an underlying difference between a financial arrangement in which monies are allocated and expenses must be controlled in order to remain within the allocation, even when the allocation may in fact be cut or, wonder of wonders increased, and a financial situation where activity generates revenue and revenue is therefore dependent upon satisfactory marketing and market conditions. In the latter instance, the agency has some control over both sides of the budget. Not only is it possible to reduce expenses in order to come out even, but there is also the option of increasing revenues. However, should market conditions cause a decline in revenues, there is no higher power to whom to appeal for a larger allocation. One simply must cut the expense budget in order to reach the end of the year without being in the red. The unfortunate aspect of the fact that librarians work in an allocation situation is that they frequently do not understand that operating funds for companies and for networks are not allocated; they must be earned. While it is true that governmentally supported networks may be subsidized so as to save members the operating costs, the not-for-profit organization must generate its revenue. This may be done through membership fees, other fees, and the pricing of products and services. Most network members pay a great deal of attention to the expense budget of their networks. Indeed, these budgets sometimes contain items for which librarians may not be accustomed to budgeting, such as telephone, rent, printing costs, travel, exhibition expenses, and the purchase of office supplies and maintenance of equipment. Rather than being subsumed in the overhead of a larger organization, networks must pay these charges on a day-to-day basis. However, equally important, and often neglected in such a review, is the revenue side of the network budget. Generating new revenues for the network is a difficult task and is always something of a gambling game. Moreover, technological developments are constantly causing network staffs to reevaluate their estimates of the revenue that will be generated from the services presently provided. The management of a network is in some ways very much like the running of a small business.

In order to manage well, one must understand what are the costs of doing business. It has taken a number of years for networks to realize the true costs of the various products and services they offer to the libraries, of the labor of their staff members, and of overhead items which are not assumed by a parent institution.

At BCR, a lack of understanding of the cost of providing service and a mentality which kept people from realizing that it was not wrong to charge for services led the organization to an alarmingly negative member equity several years ago. Through careful budgeting of expenses and active marketing efforts, coupled with favorable investment rates, the BCR has been able to emerge from its in-the-red status and now faces what one board member characterized as life after debt.

In drafting its new financial policy, the BCR is trying to guard against the possibility of another unfortunate financial crisis. That policy spells out carefully a set of controls over costs, investments, budgeting, setting of prices, collection of fees, and so forth. Every network needs to have such policies and needs to enforce them consistently.

Networks have generally priced products individually, setting a surcharge on each of the products sold. Recently, several networks have moved to a system of calculating the cost of operation as a percent of cost of product, and charging a network fee equal to that percentage. The BCR board will consider adopting a new pricing strategy perhaps as soon as the next fiscal year. This strategy can make it very clear to the libraries the exact amount they are paying the network for its services, a statistic they have every right to know. It also motivates the staff to continue to reduce the publicly announced overhead figure upon which it operates.

INTERNAL MANAGEMENT

Some of the problems which arise in the internal management of a network revolve upon the specific activities undertaken. For example, the financial constraints under which the network must operate are determined by market forces outside its control. Where libraries' budgets have been severely cut back, even though cooperative services may be in greater demand and more heavily needed, the network must keep its costs low. In a period of low network resources, the containment of costs can sometimes result in seriously unfair demands on staff members. However, reductions in service are not acceptable. At risk is the network organization itself.

A further internal restraint is imposed by the heavy travel schedule of the staff members. They are required to be out of the office a great deal of the time, and when they return, often to desks loaded with work which has arrived since they left and with requests to return phone calls accumulated during their absence, they also have brought with them work from the field which they have promised to perform upon their arrival home. Moreover, it sometimes happens that just the person they need to see is now out of the office. Sometimes, months go by between opportunities to talk to a certain colleague on the BCR staff. BCR is addressing this problem through the establishment of in-house days when all staff are required to be in the office.

Not only are the staff members away a great deal, thus becoming distanced from the activity in the office and from other staff members, but they also receive heavy rewards externally. Their activities outside the office involve training, visiting, discussing problems, and giving consultative advice, all of which are received with great gratitude by the librarians in the field. Thus, a great deal of the allegiance of the network staff member is outside the walls of the office. It is extremely important that rewards from within the organization account for a meaningful part of the staff member's positive feelings about his or her work. Management must build in opportunities for staff members to communicate with one another and for rewards to accrue to the staff member from among organizational peers and superiors.

In addition, the network is operating in a field which is constantly changing, and at a very fast pace. The amount of reading and other educational activity demanded of staff members is very great. In order to be sure that staff members have the expertise that is needed by the libraries, the network must spend a certain amount of money on reading materials, including subscriptions to technical journals, and on travel expenses and registration fees for conferences and workshops which benefit not only the staff member but the library members of the network as well.

Most networks have some kind of internal committee which handles planning and decision-making. At BCR the management committee consists of five managers, the executive director, and one elected nonmanagerial staff member. Management committee meetings monitor financial progress, marketing activity, and system usage and serve as opportunities for managers to communicate to contribute ideas and to participate actively in managing the network. In addition, staff meetings are held regularly and a bulletin board is used to chart the progress of some outstanding activities. All of these are designed to help keep interest and involvement in BCR activities high among staff members.

CONTRACTING

One of the functions networks serve is as an agent for libraries in acquiring the services offered by certain vendors. In order to carry out this activity, networks must have contractual arrangements with their library members as well as with the vendors. In contracting with libraries, we are finding that a larger percentage of contracts are attracting questions and requiring additional negotiation. There was a day in which libraries made very little fuss about contracts. Nowadays everyone reads everything. That is in many ways to our advantage, but there are sometimes real problems in explaining to attorney generals and to legal officers exactly what it is that the library is buying, why it needs it, why it should buy it from us, and why one has to be concerned about how the services are used. Much of the problematic material in contracts has to do with questions about copyright and about levels of performance. These matters are time consuming and often require the services of our attorney who can sometimes negotiate directly with another attorney and come to agreement perhaps more easily than a librarian could.

Some of the vendor contract negotiations are very simple and proceed quickly. Others may be prolonged. BCR has recently negotiated contracts with SDC and with Pergamon; it annually renews its contracts with DIALOG and BRS. It is presently in the process of renegotiating a contract for OCLC services. As many of you know, the OCLC contract negotiation process has been a troublesome one. Although OCLC had notified networks months in advance that it was intending to offer a new contract rather than renewing the old one, it was not until mid-March of 1983 that the first of several drafts from OCLC was received by networks. After careful review by all the network directors, it was decided that this contract in its various versions was not acceptable to the networks. A countercontract was offered and OCLC has offered a new draft incorporating several of the objections raised by the network directors in the first round. After a period of public positioning, serious negotiations are now under way and we fully expect to have a working contract by the beginning of the new fiscal year.

The negotiation of the OCLC contract was extremely interesting in that the libraries insisted upon their right to participate in the negotiations. Despite early hopes that the 17 networks and OCLC would be able to reach basic agreement on a generalized contract, with each network then considering specifics of its own needs, libraries rose up to demand that they have a voice in the content of the contract and networks accepted their right to do so. Needless to say, this enlarged forum made the negotiations more complicated and longer. However, in general network staffs feel that that is the way librarians work and we simply must accept that. In the long run, I am certain we will have an acceptable contract for networks which libraries can live with.

At issue in the contract are the questions: How may a library or a group of libraries use the data input by OCLC member libraries? And what is the nature of the relationship between libraries and networks and between networks and OCLC? OCLC's position regarding the use of data input by libraries has softened considerably since the earliest drafts of the contract. At the present time, it is only groups of libraries whose rights to the use of data are in any way limited by the latest OCLC version of the contract. However, for networks such as AMIGOS and SOLINET which have active programs involving the use of a data base which is essentially a subset of the OCLC data base for purposes competitive to OCLC, serious negotiations need to be carried out. The desire of other groups to carry out similar programs will require considerable accommodation on both sides.

The concept of the network as an extension of its member libraries, carrying out on behalf of the libraries' activities which they could not do alone, underlies the network directors and boards' sense of "networkness." This view contrasts strongly with that of OCLC which sees networks as independent organizations set up to purchase services from vendors and resell them to libraries. Although the difference in these two positions may not seem very great, it is essential that we come to terms with the issue before the contract is finalized.

Contracting is one of the services networks provide both vendors and members. The amount of work and time networks save both vendors and members by their contracting activities is very great. Sharing of legal costs is advantageous to the libraries involved.

RESEARCH AND ACADEMIC LIBRARIES IN NETWORKS

The role of academic and research libraries in networks is extremely important, and it is the strong desire of most network managers and boards to elicit active participation from research and academic librarians.

Smaller and medium-sized academic libraries have, in fact, formed the backbone of most network activity. Of the libraries using OCLC, 51.8 percent are in academic institutions (in BCR, the percentage is 52.7). College and community college librarians are active in networks, serving on boards and committees and as delegates to the OCLC Users Council. Research librarians have also historically played an important role in network governance. The rise of RLG and its RLIN services placed research librarians in the difficult position of having to choose between their commitment to networking with their peer libraries—large research institutions with a commonality of interest in quality cataloging, resource sharing, conservation and preservation, and research-library-directed technological advances—and their sense of noblesse oblige regarding libraries in their regional networks who have a need for their collegial contributions and for access to their rich collections. Some compromises have been effected through the mechanism of tape loading membership in OCLC, allowing links to exist between smaller libraries in OCLC and the research library collections. More important, perhaps, is the active participation of the research library directors in network affairs. Their leadership is sorely needed; the sense of unity furthered by their contributions to decision-making at the network level is always appreciated. Although OCLC has established a Research Libraries Advisory Committee (RLAC) to provide them with ideas about research libraries' needs and desires, networks also need the benefit of the advice of both academic and research libraries to plan the ways in which library members can most effectively cooperate, share resources, and work together to take advantage of technological advances and cost-saving measures.

ISSUES IN NETWORKING

Some of the key issues in modern networking have already been mentioned. For example, the question of the level at which service ought to be provided for each of a number of cooperative activities remains to be answered definitively. For instance, should all vendor brokerages be carried out by a state-level network or are there economies of scale to be enjoyed by a network encompassing a certain minimum number of libraries? How do networks offering different services interact with one another? How can the library best be served—by a mixture of services provided by one agency at a single level or by a multiplicity of agencies each allowing the library certain perquisites and advantages?

We already have seen considerable governance difference between not-for-profit corporations and government-related network agencies. In addition, there may be a proliferation of private agencies which become providers of network services. What should be the role of present networks in regard to the controversy between the private and the public sector? Should they also serve the role of coordinator of a number of such services?

The actual delivery of documents to libraries and then to users has troubled automated networks for some time. Is there some way to speed the transmission of articles and books given the tremendous increase in transmission time of requests which we already enjoy? Is this speed necessary, given the cost? Are large-scale delivery services more effective and efficient than the U.S. mail service? If so, what role ought automated networks to play in the provision of such delivery?

The home delivery of information services may have a strong impact on network activity. How can networks help libraries in promoting home delivery of information services? Is there a role for the network in direct contact with the end user?

What are the barriers to cooperativeness? Are they real or only imagined? Do librarians place limits on themselves which are greater than those imposed by their institutions, or others? How can these barriers be overcome?

The very flexibility of the network may invite invidious comparisons with libraries. This can be a liability, but ought better to be turned to the advantage of the member libraries.

FUTURE OF NETWORKS

Like other institutions, networks will survive and prosper to the extent that they provide a needed service at an affordable price. While the controversy between private and public sectors may harm networks, they could and do use suppliers in both sectors. This conflict will only be harmful to networks if they become too dependent upon one supplier, whether that supplier be public or private. Most networks are actively involved today in an effort to diversify their interests; to offer a variety of services to their members so that if harm should come to one major supplier of services, the network will be able to provide the library with alternatives.

In relation to the networks which work with OCLC, there is probably minimal danger that OCLC would move to jettison them—at least overtly—for some time. At present, OCLC has some important new products on the market in the LS/2000 line. It can ill afford to antagonize libraries who have been active users of OCLC through networks. The copyright controversy has engendered much more negative reaction from librarians than anyone could have predicted. OCLC needs networks right now and is likely to continue using them, at least for some time to come. However, it would be foolish not to recognize that alternatives to OCLC shared cataloging services exist; OCLC has spent considerable time, effort, and money in developing supplemental services which can eventually replace the revenue now generated by First Time Uses (FTUs). As the FTU revenue decreases, networks need even more to look for alternative sources of revenue-generating service.

Some of these alternatives involve the new technology. Networks are staffing up with librarians whose knowledge of technology stands at the disposal of their members. Networks have the capacity to supplement and complement the library's resources. Some of our most successful activities have been joint projects with our members. The ability of the networks to assist libraries with their automation problems, to be the extension of the library in the area of cooperation and automation, is the key to the future health of library networks.

11

External Contracting for Library Services

Nina T. Cohen

Why "external" contracting?

Every library worker knows that he or she is working under a contract. For purposes of this presentation, those contractual relationships between the institution and the professional employed by that institution are considered internal contracts. They relate to professional and institutional work conditions. As used here external contracts represent a shift of emphasis from conditions of work to the work itself. An external contract has to do only with work that must be performed and that lacks anyone under internal contract to perform it.

BACKGROUND

We are only 10 years away from the large backlogs in cataloging departments. During those 10 years we have essentially, contracted out some of the tasks involved in cataloging a book. The availability, on-line, of bibliographic information has been accomplished through an external contract in which the professional cataloger has maintained local control, but some of the work has been done by another (contracted) entity.

There was a time when journals and some monographs were

bound in the library's bindery. Many of us remember the end of the era when books were ordered directly from the publisher, one title at a time. All of us have felt the need for expert opinion from outside our institutions—an external contract with a consultant.

We have accepted the book jobber, the binder, and the consultant as people who do work for us when we want the work done. Contracting out, as it has come to be called, can be viewed as a natural extension of this kind of work relationship.

Recently, some controversy has developed over the concept of hiring contractors to do library work. It stems from the famous OMB Circular A–76[1] which directs all federal executive agencies to examine activities currently performed and to determine which might be performed by commercial vendors in the private sector. Last year libraries appeared on the list of operations that were to be evaluated. This year libraries have been removed from the list (however, "cataloging books" has remained on the list). Nonetheless, the issue has been stated and it should now be discussed and understood.

Circular A–76 lists certain costs to government which should also be considered by universities: fringe benefits, contract administration, materials and supplies, and travel. However, the thrust of Circular A–76 is to abolish departments or agencies thereby reducing the total work force on federal payrolls. This emphasis dates as far back as 1955 and has been revived in one form or another in almost every administration since then. The thrust of contracting as it is developing *now* in the library community is quite different. Reductions in work force have already taken place in academic libraries. During the last 10 years, academic library staffs have been reduced by as much as 20 percent. Academic libraries now face staffing patterns that are so rigorous that there is no option to reassign staff members for short periods, and no flexibility for special projects without negative consequences elsewhere in the total library operation. Libraries are now in a positioon where work force reduction has eroded quality and started to diminish the delivery of services. Contracting for peripheral services may be a suitable alternate.

Circular A–76 has caused some consternation for another

reason. There seems to be an assumption that if a whole library were contracted out, all of the staff would be replaced. But reconsider briefly. Even if a library were to be phased out and operated by a private contractor, would it not need trained professional and support staff? Is it not likely that the same people who ran the services before would now run them for the private contractor? Is it not conceivable that the same staff would be able to earn the same or better incomes, do the same or more interesting work, and, given the flexibility of private sector decision-making, do a better job? I do not claim all those advantages are there, but I believe it to be within the realm of possibility. Circular A–76 is an overstatement, but it is also a guide to the kinds of costs and savings you should be anticipating in using a contractor's services.

Figure 11.1.
Flow Chart References, to Determine When U.S. Governmental Units May Contract for Services.

Step
No.

(1)   Examine all activities performed by the agency to determine which activities are *Governnmental functions* and must be performed by Government employees.

(2)   Those activities which are not Governmental functions are *commercial activities* and may be performed by Government employees or by contract. These activities must be *inventoried.* There are two inventory lists: one for activities of 10 or fewer FTEs and one for activities of more than 10 FTEs.

(3)   *Schedule* commercial activities on the inventory lists *for review.* The review, which is performed at least once every five years, determines whether the commercial activity will remain in-house to be performed by Government employees or be contracted out.

(4)   Determine if the activity must be performed by Government employees for *national defense* purposes. (For Department of Defense only.) If not,

(5)   Determine if it must be performed in-house because the agency's chief medical director determines it is needed to maintain the quality of direct *patient care* in Government-operated hospitals. If not,

(6)   Determine if performance by Government employees is necessary because there is *no satisfactory commercial source* to do the work,

(7)   Or an *unacceptable delay* would occur. If not,

(8)   Determine if function should be contracted, without a cost study, under a mandatory source program or non-competitive preferential procurement program in accordance with applicable regulations. If so, convert to contract. If not,

(9)   Determine if the activity employs *10 or fewer FTEs*. If so, go to Step 11 below. If the activity is *greater* than 10 FTEs, then

(10)   Determine if it is appropriate to *waive the requirement* for a cost comparison (requires approval of persons designated per paragraph 9.a. of the Circular) and go directly to contract. If assistant secretary waiver is not obtained, go to Step 12 below.

(11)   Determine if *meaningful and effective private sector competition* will ensure reasonable prices. If so, award a contract. If not,

(12)   Perform a *cost comparison* of in-house versus contract costs in accordance with Parts II, III, and IV of this Supplement.

(13)   If the total contract costs are less than the total in-house cost estimate by *10 percent* of Government personnel costs (differential), *then award a contract. If not, the activity remains in-house* to be performed by Government employees in accordance with the reorganization plan.

Source: OMB Circular No. A-76

Figure 11.2
Flow Chart: Implementation of OMB Circular No. A-76, Existing
Government Activities and Expansions

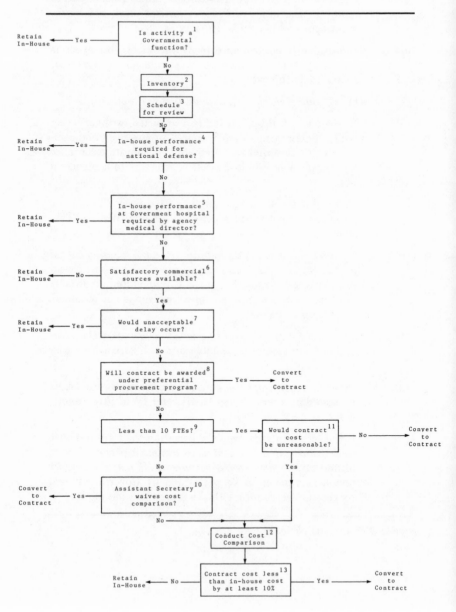

APPROPRIATE PROJECTS

If we have successfully separated the issues initially raised in Circular A–76 from the conditions presently in place, it may be possible to examine more calmly the projects that are appropriate for contracting. There are three basic categories: short-term projects, on-going (labor-intensive) operations, and experimental projects.

Short-term projects include all backlogs and overloads such as: retrospective conversion, shelving, shelf-reading, preparation of interlibrary loan and acquisition orders, clearing overdue records, and checking invoices. Less related to backlogs would be such inherently overloading operations as bindery preparation, reserve lists, term paper clinics, and inventory. The automatic, if infrequent, overloads represented by moving whole collections, starting a new branch, or merging collections are, of course, prime candidates for contracting.

Ongoing operations. At least one large university library contracts out its entire interlibrary borrowing operation. (Note that the borrowing operation demands no decision-making, simply the preparation and search operations carried out in a systematic, professional manner.) Other projects that demand some supervision and minimally trained staff include checking holdings in a card or on-line catalog as an adjunct to telephone reference activity, operation of a storage unit, and searching for materials not found on shelves by patrons. Coin-operated photocopiers are almost totally contract controlled. Many libraries run an "on demand" photocopy center through a private contractor.

Experimental projects represent projects designed to deliver to the contracting library hard, verifiable facts about an unknown operation. A contract would ordinarily be used to support or reject a newly developed technology, or it might even be used in support of cooperative projects emerging from newly formed consortia. The project is short-term and requires personnel that are not normally part of the library staffing.

Appropriate contracting usually involves both professional and support staff; the period covered by a contract is relatively short; the results are measurable; the staffing is appropriate to the specific task; the finite character of the task makes the contractor responsible for delivering results that can be evaluated.

HOW THE CONTRACTOR AND THE
ACADEMIC LIBRARY WORK TOGETHER

To obtain optimal results from the design of traditional library operation there are some guidelines that may save time and money as well as assure the success of contracting for work. Many of the articles that have appeared within the last year (several in 1983 on contracting for automation programs in *Library Journal*, for example), are valid for contracting of any kind. The examples that are discussed here are unique to contracting for overload and backlogs of ongoing work of traditional operations, where automation is not usually a cause or result and where the labor force to do the task is not available within the library.

Two processes are crucial to the success of a contractual relationship. The first has to do with conditions within the library; the other involves the process of developing and detailing the work that must be accomplished.

Academic library staffs have experienced considerable change during the last decade. They have been through the traumas of cut budgets, automation, reorganizations, self-studies, and other progressive and/or necessary change-related activities. They appear to have adjusted to the changes. But, in truth, they are extremely sensitive to possible further upheaval or infringements on territory. They are also quite defensive about backlogs or special projects that need attention. When a contractor appears on the scene, an uninformed staff will react as if it were a reflection on the efforts that they have made to keep up with the workload. An administrator, therefore, must be very sure the contract is necessary and must involve staff before the contract is under discussion. This issue is clearly related to loss of control and the feeling that middle management would retain responsibility for the operation without authority over the procedures or personnel. Had the issue been identified, it would become apparent that middle management has total control and is, indeed, responsible for final evaluation of the project and approval for the contractor's fee. Loss of control and encroachment on territory are still issues that must be openly reviewed before there will be staff cooperation, consensus, and approval.

The process of developing a contract is somewhat easier to deal with. Usually the contractor is made aware of the problem, the time constraints, and the departments involved in much the same manner that we work with consultants. The contractor works out some alternate procedures, roughs out prices and costs, and presents the library with a draft document. The draft is simply a tool to be used for precise definition of the tasks, the procedures, the working relationships, and the costs. The dialogue involved in refining the draft is the beginning of the working relationship. Once the document is agreed on by library, university, and contractor, implementation becomes a routine operation. The more complicated the project, the longer this dialogue takes. Sometimes it is easier to break down the project and negotiate it in parts as contractor and library units become more familiar with one another. Time constraints are almost as important in traditional work contracts as they are in automation contracts. The cost of contracts often depends on the speed and accuracy clauses built into the contract.

BUDGET

There are some tangible savings in working with an outside contractor and many intangible savings. The actual dollar savings are those saved by using personnel for whom no fringe benefits are paid, (15–30 percent), and for whom no overhead is incurred for such things as keeping hourly records, payroll deductions, training and scheduling. Supervisory staff is completely free of responsibility for the contracting work force. Full-time staff is no longer needed to cover seasonal or backlog workloads. The library-patron relationships that represent your best investment in next year's budget allocations can be preserved. It becomes possible to say yes to a short-term project and to accomplish it quickly without disrupting your usual services. You can add services for which you do not have to add full-time staff.

A *sample scenario*: A storage unit holding 500,000 volumes is now two years old. It is located two miles from the main library. For the most part, it needs access four to five times a week, totally unpredictably. Ordinarily, an hourly worker is sent on a special errand to pick up material. But lately it's taking a very long time—as much as 1.5 hours—to retrieve one request. Materials that need photocopying take much longer. So, in addition to the $4.50/hour for one hourly worker, you now find you must hire at least one other $4.50/hour person to accomplish the shelving that the first worker would have done. It's beginning to cost $40–$60/week. No shelving or shelf reading has been scheduled in the storage facility during the last year which has resulted in pockets of chaos. Soon, special attention will be necessary just to straighten the collection and shelve materials. A contractor can staff that facility, deliver your materials, photocopy what needs to be loaned, stack books that are returned, and read shelves for no more than $50.00/week. Your patrons and staff have predictable service with no interruption of work schedules. The contractor, by taking advantage of the flexibility of pay and time schedules available for projects that are unrelated to the "normal" work day, realizes cost plus 20 percent.

Most university library budgets include an undefined contractual services line item. Where the specific line item doesn't appear, the administrator is encouraged to apply for funds to cover contractual agreements. Contract project requests are attractive to academic administrations, especially when the contract avoids the necessity for full-time additional staffing.

Budgets for projects vary as much as libraries themselves vary. But in each contract there should be some identifiable savings to your institution in money, time, or improved services. Sometimes the value to the library is in good public relations, such as added services to the community in which you're located. In any case, if the value isn't identifiable, don't contract.

ADVANTAGES AND DISADVANTAGES

Table 11.1 is a brief summary of the now-known advantages and disadvantages of contracting externally for parts of library operations. There is no body of literature developed yet. Costs are still highly dependent on competent, knowledgeable, experienced librarians. As librarians and contractors develop facility with the processes and skills involved in defining precise and complete contracts, there will undoubtedly be discussion, approval, disapproval, constructive evaluation, and even some data.

Table 11.1
External Contracting

Advtantages	Disadvantages
I. Predictable completion	I. Request for project funds
II. Defined tasks and controlled costs	II. Time and effort to overcome staff apprehension over loss of control
III. Complete freedom from record keeping, scheduling, reassignment of staff	III. Time and effort to establish proper contract perimeters
IV. Uninterrupted operation of library services	
V. Savings to library of fringe benefits, overhead, training costs	
VI. Library staff kept at professional, highly valued tasks while contracted work is performed by others	

THE FUTURE

There are indications that library buildings will soon house the public services staff, the tools for accessing various kinds of bibliographic data, the library materials (hard copy, or otherwise), and the library user. All "input" work may be done from spaces quite distant from the library building. Will the jobber worry about what terminal was used to produce his order? Will the patron wonder why his overdue notice came from Denver? Given the decreasing need for housing some operations within the building from which we obtain or transfer information, the potential for contracting clerical and other support operations becomes somewhat greater. For those now working at some tasks within the library there will still be work, perhaps under conditions they themselves can design. There will be no need to work between 9:00 A.M. and 5:00 P.M.. One can do the work at 3:00 A.M. if it's more convenient. The workplace may become a facility designed to suit the worker and the work rather than one that serves several diverse work needs. The potential for improved productivity may at last match the potential for improved conditions of work. What appears now to be a loss of control may result in much more quality control combined with diminished effort and greater flexibility.

Perhaps that is what external contracting really is.

NOTES

1. United States Office of Budget and Management, Circular No. A–76 (Revised), August 4, 1983.

12

Taking Money for Granted: How to Attract Donor Dollars with Style and Confidence

Theodore F. Welch

After a little more than a decade of attempts at self-help in the grantsmanship process, the academic library is developing its ability to compete successfully for external funds. As librarians on campuses see their image shift from major consumers of institutional funds to that of producers of income available from a philanthropic marketplace, they also see that, as partners and competitors with campus development officers and research faculty, they are gaining the confidence and style needed to go beyond the basics of fund-raising. Armed now with information and experience that is helpful in approaching the major sources of funds—including individuals, foundations (characterized by geographic restrictions, giving emphases, and levels of support), government agencies (federal, state, and local), and corporations—librarians seek to sharpen their competitive edge in the quest for public and private funds. Mastering the art of grantsmanship involves finding and keeping individual donors, coping with the organizational problems and opportunities of support groups, learning estate and other planned giving techniques, as well as skillful preparation and delivery of proposals. Finally, knowing well the nuances applicable to the protocols (how and when to break the established rules) of fund-raising is of primary concern to those charged with successful financial development of academic libraries.

A DECADE OF PROGRESS

Although the activity of fund-raising for academic institutions is by now decades old, it was not until the late 1950s and, especially, the 1960s that grantsmanship matured on the campuses of America. Libraries were certainly the beneficiaries, albeit indirectly, of much of the external funding brought to academia. It was not until the decade of the 1970s, however, that the profession witnessed a conscious effort nationwide on the part of libraries to achieve the status of respected, well-organized, library-specific fund-raising aimed at all of the major sources of giving in the United States and abroad. It is the decade or so represented by the period of 1972 to 1982 which most clearly reflects the progress of librarianship as it has successfully embraced grantsmanship.

THE NATIONAL PATTERN OF GIVING: EDUCATION AND LIBRARIES

A look at the levels of giving in the United States by major categories will provide both the profile of giving in America as well as the trend line against which the record of library fundraising can be charted over the past decade.

Since 1972, when the total dollars given by Americans in the private sector to charitable causes was $23.3 billion, the figure has risen in 1982 to $60.39 billion, representing a growth of 159 percent. Yet, the percentage of the GNP over this period of giving has resulted in a decline from 2.01 to 1.97 percent. Of the $60.39 billion given in 1982, the distribution is as follows, in billions of dollars.[1]

Religion	$28.06	46.5%
Education	8.59	14.2%
Health/Hosp	8.41	13.9%
Social Welfare	6.33	10.5%
Arts/Humanities	4.96	8.2%
Civic & Public	2.37	2.8%
Other	1.67	3.9%

Figure 12.1
Private Sector Total Giving; from Giving USA: 1983 Annual Report

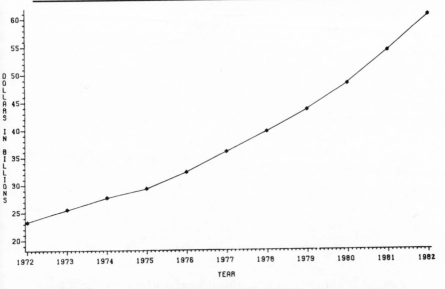

Although nearly half of all contributions and grants go to religions and religious institutions, it is clear that libraries and higher education benefit beyond the amounts and percentages indicated under "Education" in the distribution schedule.

Gifts from living individuals, bequests, foundations, and corporations, while directed primarily to one of the sectors, create a spillover effect for education and libraries. For example, of the 37 largest bequests in 1982, which ranged from a high of $1.3 billion to a low of $1 million, 35 were made to colleges and universities. Some of the recipients were religious institutions which support education, others were medical facilities attached to educational organizations, and one was to the New York Public Library, a well-established research institute in its own right. The subject distribution of grants made by foundations shows that the largest share went to welfare, followed by education, health, cultural activities, social science, science, and, lastly, religion. It is important to note that, *by type of organization*, the foundations made 42.5

Figure 12.2
Giving by Corporations, Foundations, and Bequests; from Giving
USA: 1983 Annual Report

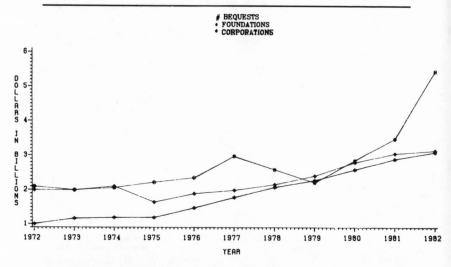

percent of these grants to educational institutions, for a total
in 1982 of $634,527,836.

Libraries received $26,511,466, representing a percentage
share of 1.8. From these figures alone, however, it is difficult
to know to what extent "education" dollars were used to support libraries, and "library" dollars were spent in academic or
research libraries, as opposed to public or special libraries.

According to the records of the Association of Research Libraries, there are between 50 and 60 private foundations which
regularly give to libraries in higher education. There has been
a tendency, in the past few years, for the large foundations to
give either to the Council on Library Resources or to the Research Libraries Group. In doing so the large foundations im-
ply that these two not-for-profit organizations represent the
needs of the library profession in serving the major academic
and research activities of the nation. Originally funded by the
Ford Foundation, the Council on Library Resources (CLR) receives and distributes funds to advance public welfare by trying
to identify and contribute to the solution of problems of na-

tional and international importance. Grants primarily to institutions for experimental, demonstration, and developmental efforts that are likely to produce significant advances in the diverse fields of interest to library development are the worthy goals of this Washington, D.C.-based foundation.

Although not a foundation, the Research Libraries Group (RLG) is a consortium of about 30 research libraries in America which have developed a nationally accessible bibliographic utility and engage in a number of unique cooperative projects that address the practical issues of current librarianship. It is based in Palo Alto, California.

There are more than two hundred research libraries today which compete with these two agencies in seeking funds. Clearly, the more tried-and-true libraries with well known programs do the best when seeking funds from either the CLR or the foundations which support CLR and RLG.

GOVERNMENT PROGRAMS

The federal and state governments have been the major sources of funding for education and libraries in the past. Currently, about $15 billion, or twice the nominal amount targeted in the private sector, go to education and libraries; $6.65 billion of that figure is for libraries. Among the significant areas of support for libraries in higher education are the Higher Education Act and the Library Services and Construction Act.

The Higher Education Act (HEA) of 1965 has three sections of interest to academic libraries: Title II-A, II-B, and II-C. The College Library Resources Program (Title II-A) is intended to assist in the acquisition of library materials; the most recent level of funding stood at $1.92 million. There is no appropriation for the current year (1984) for the Title II-A program, owing to the review underway in Congress as to its usefulness. Under the provisions of Title II-B, the "Library Research and Demonstration Program" funds both contracts and grants for the purpose of improvement of library and information science practices and principles. Past grants under this program have been less than $100,000 per award, totalling $880,000 in 1982.

Figure 12.3
Giving to Education, 1978–82; from Giving USA: 1983 Annual
Report

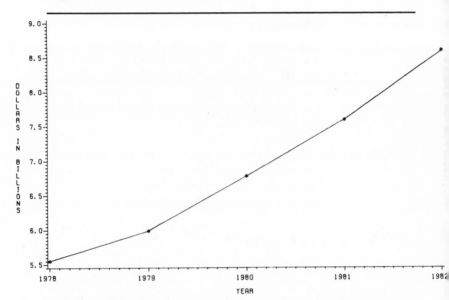

By far the largest HEA program aimed specifically at academic libraries has been the Title II-C program, "Strength-
ening Research Library Resources." The purpose of the act is
to help major research libraries maintain and strengthen their
collections, and to assist in making their holdings available to
other libraries and researchers. To be eligible, the research library must have material which is unique, not widely available, and in demand by scholars and researchers not connected with the applicant institution. Six million dollars
annually was available to this program in 1984, but its future
is in doubt. The present Administration has recommended no
funding for Title II-C in 1985.

In 1982 a variety of programs related to academic libraries
were funded at $130 million by the National Endowment for
the Humanities (NEH). These millions of dollars are designated annually for library humanities projects in the NEH di-
visions of Research Programs, Educational Programs, Fellow-

Figure 12.4
Giving to Academic Libraries, 1978–82; from Bowker Annual,
1978–1982

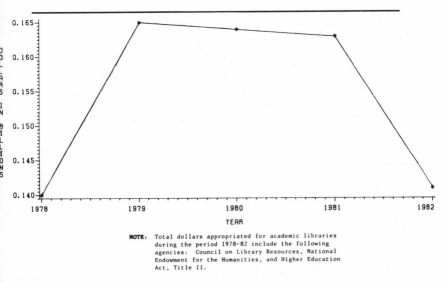

NOTE: Total dollars appropriated for academic libraries
during the period 1978-82 include the following
agencies: Council on Library Resources, National
Endowment for the Humanities, and Higher Education
Act, Title II.

ships and Seminars, as well as the General Program Division.
However, a 10 percent decrease in allocation has been recommended for 1985. The NEH Challenge Grant Program is one
of the most visionary funding activities in the public sector today. Its restrictions are few, and the latitude for creative fund-
raising it allows is a great incentive for any institution seeking a multiyear opportunity in fund-raising with a federal aid
ratio of $1 to every $3 raised from private sources.

Title III of the Library Services and Construction Act (LSCA)
deals with interlibrary cooperation. Its purpose is to provide
funding for the systematic and effective coordination of resources of school, public, academic, and special libraries. Library materials and construction are not available under this
portion of LSCA. Rather, funds are available for services and
equipment necessary for the implementation of library networks and cooperative systems. The 1982 level of funding for
this program was $11.52 million.

Some forty-five additional federal programs of possible benefit to college and university libraries, including media programs, exist. They are listed in the *Catalog of Federal Domestic Assistance*, published annually in May with two updates in September and December.

In all, there is a staggering amount of money available to academic librarianship from private and public sources. In the affluent yet highly competitive world of fund-raising, librarians are refining their strategies for greater success. Refinement assumes that sufficient initial success has been experienced by most academic libraries, and that the goal is now constant improvement leading to mastering of principles and techniques. Although it is true that a majority of libraries' basic needs are targeted in institutional budgets or met in campus-wide campaigns for capital improvement, it is also true that most libraries can benefit from independent efforts to raise monies for additional book funds, special collections, renovations, equipment, automation, staffing, preservation projects, and research.

ORGANIZING FOR DEVELOPMENT

Each university or college library that can afford it should have its own organization for fund-raising. This should be done in concert with the central campus unit for raising external funds.

On private university campuses, this is usually the office of development, administered by someone reporting directly to the president of the institution. On publicly supported campuses, this may be a quasi-independent foundation established to receive and expend external funds. These offices are generally separate from those offices on campus seeking research grants for individuals or sponsored projects that require facilitation of funding for scientific experiments.

Staffing of the library development office ideally comes from within the library organization. There must be central control on campus for external fund-raising, so as to avoid duplication of effort that might lead to needless confusion or embarrassment when uncoordinated appeals are made from the same institution. Every effort should be made to ensure that the best proposal is submitted to each donor. It follows that the library should house its own centrally controlled development office. This would presumably be in or near the offices of library administration. The director may be the chief development officer, as is the case in many academic libraries, or another individual may be designated as coordinator for the library's program. Each year sees an increase in newly created positions related to fund development. Whether a new post is created or additional responsibility assigned, someone with library experience should be appointed to the position. This assertion is based on the assumption that it is easier to teach development skills to someone familiar with libraries than library skills to a fund-raiser. Although it is true that some central development staff without prior library experience have successfully raised funds for libraries, they tend to be the exception. In general, the advantage lies with the individual who knows the library environment well and who can be most effective in presenting the library's case to donors. A joint appointment, with shared support, is a possibility, when financial and/or human resources are limited. If such a position does not already exist in the university or the library, it might be the subject of an outright or matching grant request for seed funding to establish the position itself.

THE LIBRARY DEVELOPMENT OFFICER

It is not difficult to imagine the need for more than one full-time development officer in the academic library; certainly, the opportunities to occupy fully a staff of more than one professionally trained and experienced fund-raiser exist. But it is likely that even the largest of research libraries have yet to fund more than one position. While it is essential that the coordinator have a good grasp of the full range of library needs, strengths, services, and issues of concern to potential donors, the expertise will of necessity remain general. The development of proposals, and even targeting of possible donors, naturally lies with those specialist librarians in the organization who can speak to the relevant national and local issues which impact on their particular fields of librarianship. So, it is the mission of the coordinator, or director, of development to match granting sources with fundable ideas with style, confidence, and success.

BASIC AIDS

Aiding the coordinating officer and participating staff in this task is a host of training opportunities, written materials, consultant services, professional associations, and advice from donors. Most of the training seminars have been aimed at developing basic fund-raising skills applicable to anyone in a not-for-profit institution. Increasingly, grantsmanship for educators, and librarians, has been the focus of special training seminars conducted by national consultants, regional library organizations, or library schools.

Two recent efforts have stimulated the growth of library grantsmanship. The Friends of Libraries U.S.A. (FOLUSA) is an American Library Association-affiliated forum for the exchange of ideas and experience in dealing with library support groups and volunteer activities which can benefit the academic library. National conference programs and direct membership provide the major access to the work of FOL-USA. It publishes the quarterly, *Friends of the Library National Notebook* for its members.

For those not yet familiar with the basics, or who seek reminders of the full array of opportunities, challenges, dos and don'ts of fund-raising, there are several recent books that serve the purpose well. Richard Boss's *Grant Money and How to Get It* is a useful primer.[2] *Funding Alternatives for Libraries*, by Breivik and Gibson is a compilation of helpful essays on the protocols and practices of library fund-raising.[3] For a look at government funding sources and procedures, complete with names and addresses, there is Emmett Corry's *Grants for Libraries*.[4]

In addition, the *ALA Washington Newsletter*, published by the Association's representative lobby in Washington, provides a current awareness servicie on legislation which impacts on libraries; it is especially useful to those who are already familiar with the grants programs of the federal government.[5] Many state library associations' newsletters provide a similar window on the progress of state and local legislation and other grant activities of academic libraries in the state. The ARL "SPEC Kits" of 1978 and 1983 deal with external funding issues, campaign examples, and position descriptions of some of its member libraries.[6]

REFINING FUNDING STRATEGIES

By now there are subtleties known heretofore only by the wisened fund-raiser which are part of the working manners of the library development officer. Some of these are but slight improvements on tried, tested, true, and good methods.[7] One notion that cannot be overstated is the primary importance of the individual. Both the asker and the giver are people. Good interpersonal skills are fundamental. Whether one approaches a blue-chip corporation, a large national foundation, a government agency, or a wealthy family, those reviewing the request are only human. Treating organizations as though they were people is a useful way to perceive what otherwise appears at times as a very complex task in an awesomely competitive environment. The fund-raiser must first learn the rules governing contact with institutions and their individuals, master them, and then delicately and perceptively depart from them as necessary to hone the capabilities necessary to gain and maintain success.

One well-known director of a research library takes the attitude that he is helping the donor agency when requesting a grant. This gentleman has been so successful that he has helped shape the policies of both government and independent sector donors because of his unique style. He is reputed to mix patience with affable arrogance, sometimes insisting that it is his duty to point out that the donor is obligated by law to do the best possible service to society by placing monetary resources in the hands of his library, which is most able to realize the goals of the donor. This positive power of confidence, mixed with disarming candor, is a tool not available to all of us as yet, but the mind is stretched in contemplation of its potential in our own institutions.

In the literature much is made of the concept of effective proposal writing. Certainly, it is a rare grant that is received without first a proposal justifying the need for money. In such proposals, great attention is placed on the need for funds, the carefully constructed case statement of how society is to be improved by solving a problem that the donor has somewhere indicated interest in, the credibility of the recipient, the goals and methodology of a program or project where they are integral to the proposal, and the expected product or results of the funding. Even evaluation by disinterested but knowledgeable experts is now seen to be a viable addition to the proposal. Of course, a no-frills budget is of paramount importance, and is usually looked at first by a donor. These are all basic notions, well accepted. From these, however, spring some additional values which may be overlooked. One can spend too much time predicting the behavior of a donor, whether it be an individual or an organization. Preliminary conversation, where possible, helps shape the final proposal. Some donors prefer formal, lengthy proposals. Some do not. Many small foundations do not have the staff or overhead to read and respond to lengthy, complicated proposals. Some potential recipients, fearing rejection, overdo their proposals. One vice president of a prestigious midwestern university discovered this problem and complained that the success rate of submitted proposals was over 90 percent. "What we need," he joked, "is more poorly written proposals!" The likelihood of success with less effort was no doubt partly on his mind.

Donor organizations, institutions, agencies, and individuals, acting much like human beings, have self-interest as well as community interest in mind. The stated objectives of the donor source may be one thing, and the pattern of giving another. Research and close personal attention (as much as will be tolerated) must supplement the formal pronouncements of donors. Idiosyncrasies exist and extensive records of the people who make up the donor world should be kept, and kept up to date.

It is an obvious fact that individuals, living and otherwise, give the majority of charitable dollars in America. Knowing why people give is essential to the approach and the all-important request for money. All support seeking nonprofit institutions are in competition with 300,000 other organizations seeking financial help. Only those that know why people give, and can truly aid them in creative and effective giving—so as to allow for the greatest recognition of their contributions—will come home with the bacon.

Over 27 million Americans file tax returns which claim charitable deductions. Do librarians know and understand the tax laws and the benefits that can accrue to individual donors?

Still, some other basic problems have yet to be overcome. A very successful staff member of a large development effort at Northwestern University was asked what his key to success was. Money was coming in at a much greater rate through his efforts than those of his colleagues. His answer, in part, was, "Being a successful grantee is never having to say you're sorry." He grieved that people did everything but ask for money. They prepared and planned and played around with comprehensive strategies, but often failed to set up a schedule of requests. Perhaps out of fear of being rejected by donors, especially individuals, staff would not ask. We all know of cases where the first or second request was not successful, but subsequently, donations were made which would not have been if further requests had not been made. Few of us enjoy the status that the late Dr. Roscoe Miller, President of Northwestern University, had, when he claimed, "I have never had to ask for money."

Librarians have been preoccupied in the first decade of their fund-raising experience with the basics: the mechanics, the campus politics, the pressures of deadlines, and the style and content of proposals, they can now turn their attention to attitudes and expectations, with a new respect from their campus peers. Librarians have gained a regard from the donor community as well. It is even possible that librarians could be pace-setters for excellence on their campuses. In 1975, when I was asked to be Assistant University Librarian for Development at Northwestern University, I was the first non-central development officer on campus to devote full time to fundraising. I attended development office meetings and learned a great deal.

My first proposal was funded at $1.4 million, received from the Venezuela government, for an automated bibliographic search project. The project resulted in staff expansion and considerable progress for the automated system in place at Northwestern. The grant strengthened the position of the University Library on campus, by bringing in dollars, personnel, growth, and recognition. The library enjoyed a greater sense of belonging to the university, being a producer of income rather than merely an endless consumer of university dollars. With recognition came increased voice in the decision-making processes of the university which affected the library. The library and the director had "clout." Soon, other Northwestern University colleges and departments followed suit; all now have their own development officers who coordinate their special interests with the central office, and with each other on joint projects.

Because the library, like most research libraries, has no natural constituency, such as those enjoyed by the various departments, schools, and colleges, obstacles exist for gaining access to alumni. The barriers occur both on and off campus. Yet these can be overcome if a spirit of understanding and cooperation can be achieved with campus colleagues involved with fund-raising for their specific units. The library, being less proprietary than all other academic units, should be allowed a fair share of the alumni market, with access especially to those who have known interests in libraries, even those who are nongivers to the university—those hard-core reluctant-to-give alums—have come around to a request from a library, feeling that it was one place of happy memories where no grades (only an occasional fine) were imposed. Such obstacles can be turned into opportunities by persistently increasing the viability of the library on campus through successful efforts to help itself in the external funding arena.

One objective to strive for is the much preferred unrestricted grant, rather than the restricted or programmatic fund. One ideal to aspire to is funding for what one is already doing. Instead of committing the library to take on a new set of tasks, with new staff and skills required, it is often the more desirable route to acquire monies for important programs which are already being carried out anyway. This can free institutional resources for other, not readily funded, library activities and services. The greatest source for unrestricted money is the individual donor or patron. It is also the most difficult donation to come by. The government, except in the Challenge Grant Program of the NEH, provides the least opportunity for unrestricted funds.

One final area of great potential to which librarians might usefully turn their attention is estate planning. With the assistance of legally trained development officers on campus, the living donor is increasingly attracted to life-income agreements, annuity trusts, unitrusts, charitable gift annuities, charitable-remainder annuity trusts, charitable remainder unitrusts, and other forms of deferred gifts. Most of these contributions are made during the donor's lifetime but do not accrue to the full benefit of the institution until sometime in the future, usually upon the death of the donor, his or her spouse, or income beneficiary. As librarians become familiar with these tools, and how to present them in their essence until they can be fully explained by a donor's attorney or the university legal counsel, confidence will grow.

Not all of the major fund-raising programs are suitable for each library. Awareness of the cost-benefit ratios of each type of endeavor, from capital campaigns, to leadership gifts, telethons, direct mailings, book sales, friends groups functions, in-kind donations, volunteerism, and so forth, will help avoid costly trial and error approaches. As the suitability of each endeavor is known, the ability to repeat successfully the fund-raising activities will create the confidence and style vitally needed.

NOTES

1. American Association of Fund-Raising Counsel, *Giving, USA: 1983 Annual Report* (New York: AAFRC, 1983), 96 pp.

2. Richard W. Boss, *Grant Money and How to Get It: A Handbook for Librarians* (New York: R. R. Bowker, 1980), 138 pp.

3. Patricia Senn Breivik and E. Burr Gibson, eds., *Funding Alternatives for Libraries* (Chicago: American Library Association, 1979), 174 pp.

4. Emmett Corry, *Grants for Libraries: A Guide to Public and Private Funding Programs and Proposal Writing Techniques* (Littleton, CO: Libraries Unlimited, 1982), 240 pp.

5. *ALA Washington Newsletter* (Washington, D.C.: Office of the American Library Association).

6. Association of Research Libraries, Systems and Procedures Exchange Center, *External Fund Raising in ARL Libraries: Kit 48* (Washington, D.C.: ARL, October 1978), 106 pp; Association of Research Libraries, Systems and Procedures Exchange Center, *Fund Raising in ARL Libraries: Kit 94* (Washington, D.C.: ARL, May 1983), 103 pp.

7. *Success Stories: How 15 Libraries Raised Money and Public Awareness* (Chicago: American Library Association, 1983), 52 pp.

For Further Reading

Compiled by Nancy E. Elkington

AUTOMATION

Boss, Richard W. *Automating Library Acquisitions, Issues and Outlook*. Professional Librarian Series. White Plains, NY: Knowledge Industry Publications, 1982.

Carter, Ruth C., and Bruntjen, Scott. *Data Conversion*. Professional Librarian Series. White Plains, NY: Knowledge Industry Publications, 1983.

Chen, Ching-chih, and Bressler, Stacey E., eds. *Microcomputers in Libraries*. Applications in Information Management and Technology Series. New York: Neal-Schuman, 1982.

Cline, Hugh F., and Sinnott, Loraine T. *The Electronic Library: The Impact of Automation on Academic Libraries*. Lexington Books Special Series in Libraries and Librarianship. Lexington, MA: Lexington Books, 1983.

Dudley, Edward, ed. *The Development of National Library and Information Services: Papers Given at the First Library Association International Workshop, London, 1981*. London: The Association, 1983.

Fosdick, Howard. *Structured PL/I Programming for Textual and Library Processing*. Littleton, CO: Libraries Unlimited, 1982.

Gellatly, Peter, ed. *The Management of Serials Automation: Current Technology & Strategies for Future Planning*. A Monographic Supplement to *The Serials Librarian*, vol. 6, 1981/1982. New York: Haworth Press, 1982.

Grosch, Audrey N. *Minicomputers in Libraries, 1981–82: The Era of Distributed Systems.* Professional Librarian Series. White Plains, NY: Knowledge Industry Publications, 1982.

Hagler, Ronald, and Simmons, Peter. *The Bibliographic Record and Information Technology.* Chicago: American Library Association, 1982.

Hills, Philip J., ed. *Trends in Information Transfer.* Westport, CT: Greenwood Press, 1982.

Hou, Hsieh Sheng. *Digital Document Processing.* New York: Wiley, 1983.

Ladenson, Alex, ed. *Current Trends in Library Automation: Papers Presented at a Workshop.* Sponsored by the Urban Libraries Council in cooperation with the Cleveland Public Library, May 7–8, 1981. Chicago: Urban Libraries Council, 1981.

Lancaster, F. Wilfrid. *Libraries and Librarians in an Age of Electronics.* Arlington, VA: Information Resources Press, 1982.

Matthews, Joseph R., ed. *A Reader on Choosing an Automated Library System.* Chicago: American Library Association, 1983.

Matthews, Joseph R., and Hegarty, Kevin, eds. *Automated Circulation: An Examination of Choices.* Proceedings of a pre-conference sponsored by the Circulation Services Section, Library Administration and Management Association, American Library Association, July 8–9, 1982, Philadelphia, Pennsylvania. Chicago: American Library Association, 1984.

Potter, William Gray, and Sirkin, Arlene Farber, eds. *Serials Automation for Acquisition and Inventory Control.* Papers from the Library and Information Technology Association Institute, September 4 and 5, 1980, Milwaukee, Wis. Chicago: American Library Assocation, 1981.

Reynolds, Dennis. *Library Automation: Issues and Applications.* New York: Bowker, 1984.

Saffady, William. *Introduction to Automation for Librarians.* Chicago: American Library Assocation, 1983.

Thompson, James. *The End of Libraries.* London: Bingley, 1982.

Woods, Lawrence A., and Pope, Nolan F. *The Librarians' Guide to Microcomputer Technology and Applications.* White Plains, NY: Knowledge Industry Publications, 1983.

COOPERATIVE VENTURES

Knievel, Helen A., ed. *Cooperative Services: A Guide to Policies and Procedures in Library Systems.* New York: Neal-Schuman, 1982.

Luquire, Wilson, ed. *Library Networking—Current Problems and Fu-*

ture Prospects: Papers Based on the Symposium "Networking, Where from Here?" New York: Haworth Press, 1983.

Markuson, Barbara Evans, and Woolls, Blanche, eds. *Networks for Networkers: Critical Issues in Co-operative Library Development.* Conference on Networks for Networkers, Indianapolis, 1979. Sponsored by the U.S. Office of Education, Office of Library and Learning Resources. New York: Neal-Schuman, 1980.

Patrick, Ruth J.; Casey, Joseph; and Novalis, Carol M. *A Study of Library Cooperatives, Networks, and Demonstration Projects.* New York: K. G. Saur, 1981.

Patrick, Ruth J.; Casey, Joseph; and Novalis, Carol M. *A Study of Library Cooperatives, Networks, and Demonstration Projects: Final Report.* New York: K. G. Saur, 1980.

COST OF SERVICES

Chen, Ching-chih, and Hernon, Peter. *Information Seeking: Assessing and Anticipating User Needs.* Applications in Information Management and Technology Series. New York: Neal-Schuman, 1982.

Dewey, Patrick R. *Public Access Microcomputers: A Handbook for Librarians.* Professional Librarian Series. White Plains, NY: Knowledge Industry Publications, 1984.

Divilbiss, James. L., ed. *Public Access to Library Automation/Clinic on Library Applications of Data Processing, 1980.* Champaign, IL: University of Illinois School of Library and Information Science Publications Office, 1981.

Drake, Miriam, ed. *User Fees: A Practical Perspective.* Littleton, CO: Libraries Unlimited, 1981.

Gates, Jean Key. *Guide to the Use of Libraries and Information Sources.* 5th ed. New York: McGraw-Hill, 1983.

Hernon, Peter, ed. *Collection Development and Public Access of Government Documents: Proceedings of the First Annual Library Government Documents and Information Conference.* Held in Boston, MA, March 3–4, 1981. Westport, CT: Meckler, 1982.

Hernon, Peter, and McClure, Charles R. *Public Access to Government Information: Issues, Trends and Strategies.* Libraries and Information Science Series. Norwood, NJ: Ablex Publishing Corp., 1984.

Hyman, Richard Joseph. *Shelf Access in Libraries.* ALA Studies in Librarianship, no. 9. Chicago: American Library Association, 1982.

Kibirige, Harry M. *The Information Dilemma: A Critical Analysis of*

Information Pricing and the Fees Controversy. New Directions in Librarianship, no. 4. Westport, CT: Greenwood Press, 1983.

Maranjian, Lorig, and Boss, Richard W. *Fee-Based Information Services.* Information Management Series. New York: Bowker, 1980.

Myers, Marcia J., and Jirjees, Jassim M. *The Accuracy of Telephone-Based Reference/Information Services in Academic Libraries: Two Studies.* Metuchen, NJ: Scarecrow Press, 1983.

Robotham, John S., and Shields, Gerald R. *Freedom of Access to Library Materials.* New York: Neal-Schuman, 1982.

FINANCIAL PLANNING

Alley, Brian, and Cargill, Jennifer. *Keeping Track of What You Spend: The Librarian's Guide to Simple Bookkeeping.* Phoenix, AZ: Oryx Press, 1982.

Harvey, John F., and Spyers-Duran, Peter, eds. *Austerity Management in Academic Libraries.* Metuchen, NJ: Scarecrow Press, 1984.

Hayes, Sherman. "What Does It Really Cost to Run Your Library?" *Journal of Library Administration* 1 (2): 1–10 (1980).

Johnson, Edward R. "Financial Planning Needs of Publicly-Supported Academic Libraries in the 1980s: Politics as Usual." *Journal of Library Administration* 3 (3/4): 23–36 (1982).

Martin, Murray S., ed. *Financial Planning for Libraries.* New York: Haworth Press, 1983.

McClure, Charles R., ed. *Planning for Library Services: A Guide to Utilizing Planning Methods for Library Management.* New York: Haworth Press, 1982.

Prentice, Ann E. *Financial Planning for Libraries.* Scarecrow Library Administration Series, no. 8. Metuchen, NJ: Scarecrow Press, 1983.

Spyers-Duran, Peter. "Prediction of Resource Needs: A Model Budget Formula for Upper Division University Libraries." Ed.D. diss., Nova University, 1975.

———. "Proposed Model Budget Analysis System and Quantitative Standards for the Libraries of the Nebraska State Colleges." Boca Raton, FL: the Author, ERIC Document Reproduction Service No. ED 077 529.

FUNDRAISING AND LIBRARY SUPPORT

Association of Research Libraries, Systems and Procedures Exchange Center. *External Fund Raising in ARL Libraries.* Spec

Kit 48. Washington, DC: Association of Research Libraries, October 1978.

Association of Research Libraries, Systems and Procedures Exchange Center. *Fund Raising in ARL Libraries*. Spec Kit 94. Washington, DC: Assocation of Research Libraries, May 1983.

Boss, Richard W. *Grant Money and How to Get It: A Handbook for Librarians*. New York: Bowker, 1980.

Brakely, George A. *Tested Ways to Successful Fund-Raising*. New York: American Management Association, 1980.

Breivik, Patricia S., ed. *Funding Alternatives for Libraries*. Chicago: American Library Association, 1979.

Broce, Thomas E. *Fund-Raising, the Guide to Raising Money from Private Sources*. Norman, OK: University of Oklahoma Press, 1979.

Buckman, Thomas R., and Goldstein, Sherry E. "Foundation Funding." In *Funding Alternatives for Libraries*, edited by Patricia S. Breivik. Chicago: American Library Association, 1979.

Corry, Emmett. *Grants for Libraries: A Guide to Public and Private Funding Programs and Proposal Writing Techniques*. Littleton, CO: Libraries Unlimited, 1982.

Cumerford, William. *Fund-Raising: A Professional Guide*. Fort Lauderdale, FL: Ferguson E. Peters Co., 1978.

Dolnick, Sandy, ed. *Friends of Libraries Sourcebook*. Chicago: American Library Association, 1981.

Flanagan, Joan. *The Grass Roots Fund-Raising Book*. Chicago: The Swallow Press, 1977.

Hill, William J. *Successful Grantsmanship*. Steamboat Springs, CO: Grant Development Institute, 1980.

Krummel, Donald W., ed. *Organizing the Library's Support: Donors, Volunteers, Friends*. Papers presented at the Allerton Park Institute sponsored by University of Illinois, Graduate School of Library Science, held November 11–14, 1979, Allerton House, Monticello, Illinois. Champaign, IL: University of Illinois, Graduate School of Library and Information Science Publications Office, 1980.

Lane, Alfred H. *Gifts and Exchange Manual*. Westport, CT: Greenwood Press, 1980.

Leerburger, Benedict A. *Marketing the Library*. Professional Librarian Series. White Plains, NY: Knowledge Industry Publications, 1981.

Mosher, Paul. "Friends Groups and Academic Libraries." In *Organizing the Library's Support: Donors, Volunteers, Friends*, edited by Donald W. Krummel. Champaign, IL: University of Illinois,

Graduate School of Library Science and Information Science Publications Office, 1980.

Pulling, Lisa. *The KRC Desk Book for Fund-Raisers: With Model Forms and Records*. New Canaan, CT: KRC Development Council, 1980.

Rosenzweig, Robert. *The Research Universities and Their Patrons*. Berkeley, CA: University of California Press, 1982.

Success Stories: How 15 Libraries Raised Money and Public Awareness. Chicago: American Library Association, 1983.

Sweeney, Robert D. *Raising Money through Gift Clubs*. Washington, DC: Council for Advancement and Support of Education, 1982.

Winning the Money Game: A Guide to Community Based Library Fundraising. New York: Baker and Taylor, 1979.

INFORMATION SYSTEMS AND SERVICES

Christie Bruce. *Face to File Communication: A Psychological Approach to Information Systems*. Wiley Series in Information Processing. Chichester, England, and New York: J. Wiley, 1981.

Gerrie, Brenda. *Online Information Systems: Use and Operating Characteristics, Limitations, and Design Alternatives*. Arlington, VA: Information Resources Press, 1983.

Keren, Carl, and Perlmutter, Linda, eds. *The Application of Mini- and Micro-Computers in Information, Documentation, and Libraries*. Proceedings of the International Conference on the Application of Mini- and Micro-Computers in Information, Documentation, and Libraries, Tel-Aviv, Israel, March 13–18, 1983. New York: North Holland Publishing Company, distributed by Elsevier Science Publishing Company, 1983.

Kruzas, Anthony T., and Schmittroth, John Jr., eds. *Encyclopedia of Information Systems and Services*. Detroit, MI: Gale Research, 1982.

Smith, Linda C., ed. *New Information Technologies—New Opportunities*. Paper presented at the 1981 Clinic on Library Applications of Data Processing, April 26–29, 1981. Champaign, IL: University of Illinois, Graduate School of Library and Information Science Publications Office, 1982.

Stueart, Robert D., ed. *Information Needs of the 1980s: Libraries' and Information Services' Role in "Bringing Information to People."* Based on the deliberations of the White House Conference on Library and Information Services. Foundations in Library and Information Science, vol. 15. Greenwich, CT: JAI Press, 1982.

Sweeney, G. P., ed. *Information and the Transformation of Society*. Papers from the First Joint International Conference of the Institute of Information Scientists and the American Society for Information Science, held at St. Patrick's College, Dublin, Ireland, June 28–30, 1982. New York: North Holland Publishing Co., distributed by Elsevier Science Publishing Company, 1982.

LIBRARY MANAGEMENT AND ADMINISTRATION

Anderson, A. J. *Problems in Library Management*. Library Science Text Series. Littleton, CO: Libraries Unlimited, 1981.

Bommer, Michael R. W., and Chorba, Ronald W. *Decision Making for Library Management*. The Professional Librarian Series. White Plains, NY: Knowledge Industry Publications, 1981.

Boss, Richard W. *The Library Manager's Guide to Automation*. 2d ed. White Plains, NY: Knowledge Industry Publications, 1983.

Chen, Ching-chih, ed. *Library Management without Bias*. Based on materials covered in the Institute on Library Management without Bias, April 30–May 4, 1979, held at the MIT Endicott House, Dedham, MA. Foundations in Library and Information Science, vol. 13, Greenwich, CT: JAI Press, 1980.

Closurdo, Janette S. Caputo, ed. *Library Management*. Papers from the Management Workshops sponsored by the Special Libraries Association Library Management Division during the 70th Annual Conference of the Special Libraries Association held in Honolulu, Hawaii, June 7–14, 1979. New York: Special Libraries Assocation, 1980.

Dougherty, Richard M., and Heinritz, Fred J. *Scientific Management of Library Operations*. Metuchen, NJ: Scarecrow Press, 1981.

Evans, G. Edward. *Management Techniques for Librarians*. 2d ed. Library and Information Science. New York: Academic Press, 1983.

Issues in Library Management: A Reader for the Professional Librarian. White Plains, NY: Knowledge Industry Publications, 1984.

Johnson, Edward R., and Mann, Stuart H. *Organization Development for Academic Libraries: An Evaluation of the Management Review and Analysis Program*. Contributions in Librarianship and Information Science, no. 28. Westport, CT: Greenwood Press, 1980.

Kathman, Michael D., and Massman, Virgil F., eds. *Options for the*

80s: Proceedings of the Second National Conference of the Association of College and Research Libraries. Foundations in Library and Information Science, vol. 17, pt. A. Greenwich, CT: JAI Press, 1982.

Lancaster, F. Wilfrid, ed. *Library Automation as a Source of Management Information.* Clinic on Library Applications of Data Processing, 1982. Champaign, IL: University of Illinois Graduate School of Library and Information Science Publications Office, 1983.

Lynch, Mary Jo, ed., Eckard, Helen M., project officer. *Library Data Collection Handbook.* A report prepared for the National Center for Educational Statistics. Chicago: Office for Research, American Library Association, 1981.

Martell, Charles R., Jr. *The Client-Centered Academic Library: An Organizational Model.* Contributions in Librarianship and Information Science, no. 42. Westport, CT: Greenwood Press, 1983.

Martin, Murray S. *Issues in Personnel Management.* Foundations in Library and Information Science, vol. 14. Greenwich, CT: JAI Press, 1981.

McClure, Charles R. *Information for Academic Library Decision Making: The Case for Organizational Information Management.* Contributions in Librarianship and Information Science, no. 31. Westport, CT: Greenwood Press, 1980.

McClure, Charles R., and Samuels, Alan R., eds. *Strategies for Library Administration: Concepts and Approaches.* Littleton, CO: Libraries Unlimited, 1982.

Person, Ruth J., ed. *The Management Process: A Selection of Readings for Librarians.* Chicago: American Library Association, 1983.

Riggs, Donald E., ed. *Library Leadership: Visualizing the Future.* Phoenix, AZ: Oryx Press, 1982.

Rowley, Jenny E., and Rowley, Peter J. *Operations Research: A Tool for Library Management.* Chicago: American Library Association, 1981.

Sager, Donald J. *Participatory Management in Libraries.* Scarecrow Library Administration Series, no. 3. Metuchen, NJ: Scarecrow Press, 1982.

Stevens, Norman D. *Communication throughout Libraries.* Scarecrow Library Administration Series, no. 6. Metuchen, NJ: Scarecrow Press, 1982.

About the Editors and Contributors

PETER SPYERS-DURAN has an M.A. from the University of Chicago Graduate Library School and an Ed.D. from Nova University. He is Director of Libraries, Wayne State University in Detroit. Formerly the Executive Director, California State University Library and Learning Resources, Long Beach, he has consulted and taught library science and is a former President, University of Chicago Graduate Library School Alumni Association. In the past 17 years, he has made numerous contributions as an author or editor to the literature of collection development and library management. He is an active member of ALA. In addition, Spyers-Duran is a Standing Committee member, International Federation of Library Associations and Institutions' Section on University Libraries and Other General Research Libraries.

THOMAS WILLIAM MANN, JR., received his M.A. in History and the M.S. in Library Science from the University of Illinois at Urbana. Currently on the professional management consulting staff of Peat, Marwick, Mitchell & Co. in San Francisco, he formerly served as Director of Administrative Services of the University Library and Learning Resources at California State University, Long Beach. Mann previously held an administrative position at Florida Atlantic University. He has had managerial, administrative, teaching, and technical services assignments in academic libraries. He has coedited *Shaping Library Collections for the 1980s* with Peter Spyers-Duran and is the author of *College and University Library Buildings* and other reports and publications.

NINA T. COHEN is President of Library Support Services, Inc., Pasadena, California, and has had a diverse career as a professional librarian. She has been a technical services innovator, an expert in public services, and a college and university administrator and is currently president of her own company.

NANCY E. ELKINGTON received her M.S. in Library Science from Wayne State University in 1984 and currently holds the position of Assistant Librarian, Research Library Residency Program, University of Michigan. During the preparation of this volume, she served as Research Assistant to the Director of Libraries at Wayne State University.

SIGMUND G. GINSBURG is Vice President for Finance and Treasurer at the University of Cincinnati, Cincinnati, Ohio, where he has served since 1978. He is the author of the books *Ropes for Management Success: How to Climb Higher, Faster* and *Management: An Executive Perspective* and coauthor of *Managing the Higher Education Enterprise*. His numerous articles have centered on management, finance, public and university administration, and human resources.

MAURICE GLICKSMAN is Provost and Dean of the Faculty at Brown University, Providence, Rhode Island, and received his Ph.D. in Physics from the University of Chicago in 1954. He became a Member of the Board of Directors, The Center for Research Libraries in 1981 and served as Chairman of the Board for 1983–84. He is joint author of *Microwave Solid State Engineering*.

SHERMAN HAYES is Assistant to the Director in the Chester Fritz Library of the University of North Dakota at Grand

Forks, North Dakota and has been concerned primarily with budgeting and financial planning in libraries. He is the author of "Budgeting for and Controlling the Cost of 'Other' in Library Expenditures: the Distant Relative in the Budgeting Process" and the editor of *A Primer of Business Terms Related to Libraries*.

EDWARD R. JOHNSON is Director of Libraries at North Texas State University at Denton, Texas and is also Chair for the College and University Library Division of the Texas Library Association. His recent publications include "Academic Library Planning, Self-Study and Management Review" and *Organization Development for Academic Libraries* as well as "Ralph E. Ellsworth" in *Leadership in American Academic Librarianship*.

PAUL B. KANTOR is President of Tantalus, Inc. located in Cleveland, Ohio, which he formed in 1977. With a Ph.D. in Theoretical Physics, his interests now lie in the field of Information Science and his company provides management consulting services in this area. His most recent article is "Objective Performance Measures for Academic and Research Libraries."

DANIEL W. LESTER is Director of the Library at Fort Lewis College in Durango, Colorado, and has held various offices in ALA RTSD and ALA GODORT. Since 1972, his principal interest has been academic library formulas and formula funding. Previous major publications include *Cumulative Title Index to United States Public Documents, 1789–1976* and *Checklist of U.S. Public Documents, 1789–1970*.

MURRAY S. MARTIN is University Librarian at Tufts University in Medford, Massachusetts, and has also held positions in the New Zealand National Library Service, the University of Saskatchewan, and Pennsylvania State University. His publishing record includes numerous articles and chapters on collection development and library management. He is the author of *Budgetary Controls in Academic Libraries* and *Issues in Personnel Management in Academic Libraries.*

RICHARD W. McCOY is President of Research Libraries Group, Stanford, California, and was formerly Director of the Wisconsin State Office of Information Systems Management. Holding degrees in Engineering, Management and Applied Computing, McCoy has held a variety of positions in the federal government, the state of Wisconsin, and the University of Wisconsin.

SAMUEL B. SAUL is Vice-Chancellor at the University of York at Heslington, England, and has held that position since 1978. He is the author of *Studies in British Overseas Trade 1870–1914* and *Technological Change: The US and UK in the 19th Century* and is coauthor of *The Economic Development of Continental Europe in the 19th Century.*

JOAN S. SEGAL, formerly Executive Director of The Bibliographic Center for Research, Rocky Mountain Region, Inc. at Denver, Colorado, is currently Executive Director of The Association of College and Research Libraries of the American Library Association. With her M.S. in Library Science from Columbia University and her Ph.D. in Communication from the University of Colorado, she is a leader in the field of library networking. She is coauthor of "BCR's Regional Union Catalog and Interloan Service" and author of "Managing the Cooperative Network."

DAVID C. WEBER is Director of University Libraries at Stanford University, Stanford, California. He is a former president of the Association of College and University Libraries, a founder of the RLIN automation system and represents Stanford on the Board of Governors at the Research Libraries Group. He is coauthor of the book *University Library Administration.*

THEODORE E. WELCH is Director of University Libraries at Northern Illinois University, DeKalb, Illinois, and has published extensively in both English and Japanese. Prior to being appointed Director of Libraries in 1983, he was very active in the Japanese Center for the Study of US–Japan Relations. His principal work is *Toshokan: Libraries in Japanese Society*.

Index